THE JESUIT MARTYRS
OF
EL SALVADOR:

CELEBRATING
THE
ANNIVERSARIES

Louie,

In friendship &
solidarity.

Joe

THE JESUIT MARTYRS
OF EL SALVADOR:
CELEBRATING THE ANNIVERSARIES

Joseph E. Mulligan, S.J.

FORTKAMP PUBLISHING COMPANY
BALTIMORE, MARYLAND

ISBN: 1-879175-15-0

LCCN: 94-061275

Laser Typography by Elizabeth Dunbar, Baltimore, Maryland

FORTKAMP PUBLISHING COMPANY
202 Edgevale Road
Baltimore, Maryland 21210
1-800-43-PEACE
1-800-437-3223

ACKNOWLEDGMENTS

We wish to express our gratitude to Mark Danner for permission to quote from his book, *The Massacre at El Mozote* (New York: Vintage Books, 1994); to the Lawyers Committee for Human Rights for permission to use material from Martha Doggett's *Death Foretold: The Jesuit Murders in El Salvador* (Washington, D.C.: Georgetown University Press, 1993); to the Permanent Committee on the National Debate in El Salvador for permission to use the award-winning poster which is on the cover of this book; and to Dr. Michael McGuire of Incarnate Word College in San Antonio, Texas, for his pictures showing the damage done to the UCA's Center for Theological Reflection.

CONTENTS

PREFACE

In November 1990, in the midst of war and with the pain of loss still fresh, we celebrated the first anniversary of the UCA martyrs. Still, the anniversary was a time not simply to share loss but to share faith and hope as well. For if these eight, like so many thousands, could give their lives for the truth, for the poor, for God, then we all had more reason to go on living and struggling for life. We had more reason for not allowing hatred and death to have the last word.

The days following the commemoration at the university led many of us into the countryside for further remembrance. At a vigil near Jayaque, where Nacho Martin-Baró had spent a lot of time, Teresa Pérez, an elderly catechist and community leader, took the floor after the Gospel reading. Standing erect in her simple cotton dress and white apron, eyes flashing from her dark brown face, Teresa reminded people how, following Padre Nacho's death, a large number had left the parish. (In fact, the army had turned the chapel where we were celebrating into a barracks for six weeks.) Teresa had a different outlook. 'Well, I say," she continued, 'if death finds us here serving the church, then let's welcome it!"

Teresa exemplifies the type of faith which has justly made El Salvador a symbol of what the church can and should be in our time. If the world has been shocked by the torture and murder of Salvadoran civilians, it has also been caught up short, inspired, by the faith of the people. They remember the famous martyrs, Archbishop Romero and the Jesuits, most of all. Still, neither Archbishop Romero nor the Jesuits fell from the sky. They fed on the faith of the Salvadoran poor with whom they mixed their blood. That faith continues to take one's breath away. It is a faith worth sharing, as this book admirably shares it.

❄   ❄   ❄

Five years after the UCA murders, a constant stream of visitors from all over continues to pass through the Pastoral Center at the university and the rose garden where the martyrs fell. Even atheists come as pilgrims. They have broken with the familiar to come to poor countries where many have given their lives for others. They're looking for reasons to hope in a violent and cynical world.

The visitors de-plane a bit anxious; they vaguely dread what awaits them in El Salvador. Aware that the people are very poor, that they have suffered torture, massacres and bombings, the visitors harbor a vague fear that the people might lunge for their first-world wallets, or that they will suffer a massive guilt attack when they visit their first poor community. Or they fear half-consciously that the visit will force them to rush back home and sell their VCRs.

Well, as happens with most fears, it doesn't turn out that way. It is not that the suffering isn't there. It's just that the Salvadoran poor are genuinely glad they have come and receive them without questions and with open arms. Of course, if the pilgrims have the courage to listen to the stories of weeks of flight from the army, of the death squads and the terror, of the bombings and the hunger, of the premature death, the people will break their hearts.

That, after all, is the main reason the pilgrims have come: to have these people break their hearts. Part of them would resist. After all, the people have the capacity to blow your world apart. My God, babies die from preventable disease. The powerful steal from the poor at will. There is no justice. And then, what has *my* government been doing here in my name?

As the people tell their stories, you feel yourself losing control; or better, you feel the world losing its grip on you. What world? The world made up of important people like us and unimportant, poor people like them. It is a little scary. But it's essential to let the truth crash in. This is the truth that sets us free. It includes not just the suffering of the poor, but the jarring realization that they are people just like us. If the visitors allow the eyes of the poor to meet theirs, they will see their own reflection.

So, the encounter, unsettling, is a kind of falling in love. The listeners feel the earth tremble underfoot. Their horizon is opening up. They experience a sweet shame and a holy confusion which has nothing to do with paralyzing guilt or remorse. Yet in their shakenness, they feel strangely at home, accepted—even before they have cleaned up their act with these people or with billions like them.

It's not that the poor are all saints or cuddly. They can be just as petty and selfish as the rich. The point is that they are just like us and don't deserve to suffer this injustice. Those who have the courage to let this turn them upside down find themselves standing before the central drama of life.

Probably more than ninety-five percent of all the people who ever lived have struggled every day to keep the household alive against the daily threat of death through hunger, illness or violence. The non-poor are a tiny minority in history; and modernity, with all its very real benefits, has removed today's non-poor more and more from this struggle for life and against death. The mixed blessing of affluence induces a kind of low-grade confusion about what is really important in life, namely life itself and love. But the encounter with the poor stops us short; it wakes up us. When we emerge from our confusion, we realize that the marginalized are really at the center of things. It is we, in Washington and New York and Paris, who are really on the fringe. The poor can free us from that illusion and place us, too, at the center of things. We clearly need the poor more than they need us.

What is the center of things? Ignacio Ellacuría once said that it seemed that the eyes of the world were fixed on Central America. He speculated that this was because the dying and rising that is the secret drama of all our lives was occurring among these suffering peoples in especially dramatic form.

This drama typically escapes us. We suspect deep down that the world is a much crueler place than we dare admit; but we fear the encounter with the poor who bring us face to face with all this evil, and we expend enormous energy shutting out this horror from our lives. If we let their stories break our hearts, however, the victims will invite us to recognize that the world is also a much more wonderful place than we dared imagine. They will reveal to us the revolution of love that God is bringing about in the world. 'Where sin abounds, grace does more abound" (Rom 5, 20).

And so, often without being able to name it, the pilgrims discover new hope. They do find sadness and sin and even desperation in El Salvador. But what really strikes them and 'ruins them for life" is something they hadn't expected: joy. After hearing the horror stories, visitors spend much of their stay wondering Why are these people smiling? and Why do they insist on sharing their last tortilla with a visiting gringo? The joy is puzzling; it does not come from comfort or decent food or good health or power, none of which the people enjoy. They have joy *in spite of everything*. Where does it come from?

The pilgrims have come up against what St. Ignatius calls "consolation without prior cause." We have no earthly explanation for this kid of joy and generosity. Only God gives joy without prior cause. The joy indicates that God is present among these people, or, as Ignatius again says, the Resurrected One is present here, typically, as the Consoler of the afflicted who gives energy to keep on going, to struggle for a new world, to hope against hope. The people then share their hope with those who come to share their pain and, in some small way, their journey. They share with others the same consolation which they have received from God (2 Cor 1,4).

Today Central America exports more hope than bananas. The hope springs from a common project in favor of life and against death. The poor express this hope in their joy and generosity—despite everything. In the rich North, one finds faith and love. One finds solidarity, too. But one finds less and less hope. There is little sense of a common project. One finds rather personal projects and lots of loneliness. Who takes seriously the gospel of consumption and non-stop entertainment? The affluent society has brought on the obvious public pain and hopelessness of the inner city and its polar reflection and counterpart in the more privatized but very real pain of the suburbs. As Ellacuría said: 'From my point of view, the United States is much worse off than Latin America, because the United States has a solution; but in my opinion, it's a bad solution, both for them and for the world in general. On the other hand, there are no solutions in Latin America, only problems; but no matter how painful that might be, it is better to have problems than to have a bad solution for history's future."[1]

Pilgrims find hope in Central America. They learn, besides, that in order to share the hope of the poor, they must first share (hear and assume) their pain. In order to appreciate the good news that God is working a slow revolution of love in history, they must first face the bad news that the world is a terribly cruel place. To have real hope, we need for the victims to break our hearts, sweep us out of control and place us before Christ crucified in the world today. We cannot appreciate the resurrection that is taking place everywhere unless we can appreciate the crucifixions that are taking place as well. In this very real paschal mystery, in the daily dying and rising of people, we encounter a crucified and rising God and the secret of life.

The UCA martyrs and people like Teresa Pérez bear this message to a world longing for good news like water in a desert. Along with the roses planted behind the Pastoral Center at the UCA, the poor-with-spirit remind us that, when we are disposed to give our lives in service to something bigger than ourselves, in service of the truth, of the poor, of God, then death loses its great sting. Love and not hatred has the last word; life triumphs even over death.

Dean Brackley, S.J.
San Salvador
July 31, 1994
Feast of St. Ignatius Loyola

---

[1] I. Ellacuría, "*Quinto Centenario. América Latina, ¿descubrimento o encubrimiento?*" *Revista Latinoamericana de Teología 21* (1990) 277. It's not a universalizable solution; therefore it's not just.

INTRODUCTION

"The first evangelization was carried out under the flag of domination," said Brazilian theologian Leonardo Boff. "The new evangelization must be carried out under the banner of liberation and must spring from the oppressed cultures themselves."[1]

The original sin of the evangelization of Latin America is "that it formed part of a project of domination and exploitation under which the indigenous populations and later the African slaves succumbed," noted Oscar Beozzo, Brazilian theologian and Church historian.[2] "The Churches became 'bad news' for the peoples of this continent. What is fitting now is an act of penance, restitution, and the resolution to give new directions to evangelization in the future."

On the positive side, Fr. Beozzo has noted: "In Latin America there has been an authentic evangelization when the struggle for justice and the proclaiming of the God of life have walked together. There can be true evangelization in the future only if the indissoluble unity of these two realities finds courageous witnesses. 'A pagan Indian who is alive is worth more than a baptized one who is dead,' said de las Casas. Four

---

[1] *Agenda Latinoamericana '92*, by Fr. José María Vigil (Managua: Ediciones Nicarao, 1991).
[2] *Ibid.*

and a half centuries later, Archbishop Romero echoed that: "The glory of God is the poor person who lives.'

After describing some of the more important struggles for justice in our time, Beozzo concluded: "Evangelization will truly be an announcement of the 'good news' if the Church commits itself to these sectors in struggle as an integral part of its mission."[3]

In this book we will meet the Jesuit martyrs of the Central American University in El Salvador and the two women assassinated with them in 1989, coming to know them through a narrative account of the first four anniversaries of their martyrdom. Their blood, like that of Romero and the four North American missionaries killed in 1980, has truly been "the seed of Christian hope and courage" and thus an evangelizing force itself.

In many instances I have chosen to present the full text of homilies, letters, and other documents in order to make these important statements available in English and in order to let the Salvadorans speak for themselves.[4]

"Evangelization" means literally "to proclaim the good news." If that proclamation is to be real and meaningful to suffering people, it

---

[3] *Carta a las Iglesias* (San Salvador: UCA), 16-31 de julio, 1992.

[4] An excellent introduction to the martyrs, with generous samplings from their writings, is *Companions of Jesus: The Jesuit Martyrs of El Salvador* (Maryknoll, NY: Orbis, 1990).

must also include "being" and "doing" the good news, that is, transforming a distressful situation into a good reality.

The term was first used by second Isaiah (Isaiah 40-55), who proclaimed "good news" to the people captive in Babylon (present-day Iraq). It was indeed good news, for it told them that their suffering was coming to an end, that they would be liberated, and that they would return to their homeland. This happened historically through the instrumentality of Cyrus the Persian, who conquered the Babylonians.

In the New Testament a central text is Luke 4:16-30, the start of Jesus' public ministry. He read from Isaiah (61:1-2), saying: "The Spirit of the Lord is upon me, for he has anointed me to bring **good news** to the poor, freedom to captives, and to the blind new sight, to set the oppressed free, and to announce the year of the Lord's favor." Jesus went on to fulfill this programmatic statement in word and deed.

When people tried to keep him in one place, he said: "I must preach the Good News of the Kingdom of God in other towns also, because that is what God sent me to do" (Luke 4:43).

Another passage frequently cited to show the meaning of the Good News and of the Kingdom of God is Luke 7:18-23, where the disciples of John the Baptist ask Jesus whether he is the long-awaited one. Jesus answered: "Go back and tell John what you have seen and heard: the blind see, the lame walk, those who suffer from dreaded skin diseases are made clean, the deaf hear, the dead are raised to life, and the Good News is preached to the poor." By his words and deeds, Jesus was making the Good News a good reality; the Kingdom was coming on earth.

Fr. Juan Antonio Estrada, S.J., a Spanish theologian, described the Good News clearly in a seminar at the Jesuit university in Managua in

August 1991: "Jesus enters into relationships with the poor, the sinners, the tax collectors, prostitutes, with those who collaborate with the Roman empire. Why? Because Jesus comes to give us a message which is **Good News** for humanity: that God is the friend of humanity who wants to restore our sense of dignity, who commits himself to the human cause, who enters into human history, and who chooses the most humiliated, the poorest and the littlest, so that we may learn to relate to one another as brothers and sisters, as sons and daughters of God. God reveals himself from below, not as the omnipotent, distant God to be feared, but the God who is close as our companion. He is the infant in Bethlehem, the savior on the cross."

The Kingdom of God is the reign of justice and peace, of brother-hood/sisterhood. Swords are changed into plowshares (Isaiah 2:4); "they do no hurt nor harm on all my holy mountain," said the Lord (Isaiah 11:9). It is the end of exploitation and oppression. Its coming in plenitude cannot be predicted or calculated or manufactured, but we do pray: "Thy Kingdom come; thy will be done on earth as it is in heaven." We struggle constantly, with the grace of God, to bring ourselves and our world closer to the Kingdom.

In February 1992 two thousand people representing Christian base communities throughout Mexico met in Ciudad Guzmán for the 14th national assembly of the communities. The theme was "Christian base communities: transforming the people by evangelizing." Eight Mexican bishops and many priests and sisters were among the participants. The love and fellowship felt by all served as a strong impetus to continue the struggle for a new society expressed in the theme of the four-day assembly.

❄   ❄   ❄

For some years now the Church has spoken officially of the need for a "new evangelization." Progressive forces in the Church insist that this "new evangelization" began with Vatican II and was launched officially in Latin America by the 1968 meeting of the continent's bishops at Medellín, Colombia. That conference spoke of "sinful structures" of exploitation, the "institutionalized violence" of the system, and the Christian duty to struggle for peace and justice.

The 1971 synod of bishops in Rome stated that work for justice is a "constitutive dimension" of evangelization. Religious orders have taken this to heart in a special way, with more and more members living among the poor and speaking out in their defense. The Jesuits have defined their mission as "the service of faith and the promotion of justice."

Before long a conservative backlash occurred, emphasizing the "spiritual" nature of evangelization, seeking to moderate the Church's "option for the poor," and accusing those working for liberation of having lost the "transcendent" aspect of their faith. Some Church officials identified the main enemy as "secularism" or other Christian churches, especially the pentecostal sects, instead of the "sinful structures" and the "institutionalized violence" which continue to grind the poor masses.

Christians working for liberation are aware of the criticisms that have been made against them and are conscious of the dangers of "horizontalism," of reducing the gospel to social and political struggle. By and large, however, they have resisted this temptation, being faithful to the call to work for "integral (holistic) liberation," that is, a liberation which includes all essential dimensions of the human being. They are struggling today to keep their Church faithful to the stirrings of the Spirit experienced in Vatican II and Medellín, faithful to its "option for the poor," faithful to the struggle which has brought martyrdom to many.

CHAPTER 1

The Martyrdom and the First Anniversary

Jesus shared human nature "so that through his death he might
destroy the devil, who has the power of death, and in this way
set free those who were slaves all their lives because of their
fear of death.... And now he can help those who are tempted,
because he himself was tempted and suffered"
(Hebrews 2:14-15,18).

The Martyrdom

The six Jesuits killed at the Central American University (UCA) in San Salvador on November 16, 1989, were not the first Jesuit martyrs in that country. Fr. Rutilio Grande, S.J., pastor in Aguilares, was assassinated on March 12, 1977, along with two lay co-workers because their practice of evangelization included a strong defense of the rights of the poor peasants.

Subsequently a right-wing terrorist group, the White Warriors Union, issued a death threat against all Jesuits working in the country. Jesuits assigned to work in El Salvador stayed, defying the threat, while some seminarians were transferred out of El Salvador to continue their studies.

Archbishop Oscar Arnulfo Romero was gunned down while celebrating Mass on March 24, 1980. The four U.S. churchwomen (Jean Donovan and Sisters Maura Clarke, Ita Ford, and Dorothy Kazel) were brutally assassinated on December 2 of that same year. And the toll continued, including some priests and thousands of lay persons killed in the proclamation and implementation of the Good News to the poor and oppressed. The UCA was frequently the object of right-wing terrorist sabotage.

The immediate background to the killing of the six Jesuits and the two women at the UCA begins with the "urban offensive" of the FMLN (Frente Farabundo Martí de Liberación Nacional, or the Farabundo Martí Coalition for National Liberation), launched on November 11, 1989.[1] With the Frente making strong inroads into San Salvador, the military high command decided that their all-out effort would include massive bombing of the neighborhoods where the Frente had support.

Within a few hours all radio stations were ordered to tie into a nationwide network, which was actually Radio Cuscatlán, the station of the

---

[1] This escalation was preceded by three important events. (1) In September and October government and FMLN representatives met in Mexico and in San José, Costa Rica, but government intransigence resulted in the failure of the talks. (2) On October 30 the FMLN attacked Joint Command headquarters; one person died and several others were wounded. (3) In response, "the government set off a powerful bomb in the offices of COMADRES (an organization of women whose family members have been killed or disappeared) while about 100 members were attending a meeting" (Martires de la UCA; San Salvador: UCA Editores, 1990); another bomb exploded in the FENASTRAS trade union federation, killing ten union leaders. For an excellent first-person account of those dramatic days, as well as reflections on Scott Wright's life and work in El Salvador, see Scott Wright, *Promised Land: Death and Life in El Salvador* (Maryknoll, NY: Orbis, 1994).

Salvadoran Armed Forces.[2] On the government controlled airwaves, callers denounced opposition political figures, labor and church leaders, and members of nongovernmental organizations often labelled "FMLN fronts."

The statements were "vitriolic and vindictive, frequently urging violence against those named....Jesuits were also singled out. Father Ignacio Ellacuría, the UCA rector, was mentioned by several callers. 'Ellacuría is a guerrilla. Cut off his head,' said one. 'Ellacuría should be spit to death,' said another. Vice-president Francisco Merino of the ruling ARENA party accused Ellacuría of 'poisoning the minds' of Salvadoran youth."[3]

Shortly after the start of the offensive, some FMLN combatants fled through the UCA campus. On November 12 a military patrol examined the scene, finding an unexploded device; the next day the military sealed the university, prohibiting the entrance or departure of anyone. Because of its proximity to several military installations, the entire neighborhood was heavily occupied by soldiers.

On November 12 police agents entered the grounds of the Loyola Center, a Jesuit retreat complex near the UCA, finding equipment for four guerrilla combatants buried on the grounds. Father Fermín Saínz said the lieutenant in charge told him, "Don't worry, Father, we're finding things like this all over the city." The lieutenant suggested that the guerrillas probably intended to retrieve the weapons the next day. President Alfredo Cristiani later told a group of visiting U.S. Jesuits

---

[2] Martha Doggett, *Death Foretold: The Jesuit Murders in El Salvador* (Washington, D.C.: Georgetown University Press, 1993) p. 38.

[3] *Ibid.*, p. 39.

that "nobody thought [the weapons] had anything to do with the Jesuits. We saw this in lots of places."

Though the soldiers never suggested that the Jesuits were complicit in hiding the arms, "U.S. and Salvadoran officials later cited the incident, offering it in justification of the November 13 search of the Jesuit residence and, in some instances, using it to imply that the Jesuits were indeed involved in the armed uprising."[4]

On November 13 the Joint Command decided to create a special security zone (which included the area around the UCA) to protect key military installations. The Military Academy was chosen as headquarters for this zone; and its director, Col. Guillermo Alfredo Benavides, was named commander.

Military commanders decided that part of the Atlacatl Battalion, an elite U.S.-trained force established in 1981 and notorious for its brutal massacres, would be called into the capital to join this Security Command. The Atlacatl commander later testified that Col. René Emilio Ponce, then head of the Joint Command (later to become a General and the Minister of Defense), ordered him to send to the capital 90 men plus the commando unit, which was placed under the orders of the Joint Command.

The 47-man commando unit of the Atlacatl Battalion was temporarily assigned to the Military Academy. On November 10, thirteen members of a U.S. Special Forces unit from Ft. Bragg, North Carolina, had commenced a training course at Atlacatl headquarters. "Among their students were these Atlacatl commandos, seven of whom were later charged with killing the Jesuits.... The training was to be

---

[4] *Ibid.*, p. 43.

provided to some 150 Atlacatl members from November 10 to 20."[5] According to a Pentagon report, the men were to receive training in these areas, among others: Combat Orders, Rapid Fire Techniques, and Practical Exercise in Combat Orders.

During the afternoon of November 11, hours before the offensive began, Salvadoran Vice-president Francisco Merino "arrived at Atlacatl Battalion headquarters in a helicopter." Atlacatl records showed that the visit lasted two hours.[6]

All of the Atlacatl men charged in the Jesuit murders took part in the training course, which was interrupted on November 13 when Col. Ponce ordered the Atlacatl commander to bring his special unit to the Military Academy. The unit's commanding officer was Lt. José Ricardo Espinoza Guerra, one of three who later led the murder mission. The lieutenants who led the unit "reported directly to the Joint Command, where they were given an order to search the Jesuit residence (see below). The fact that these lieutenants reported directly to the Joint Command and that the commandos searched the Jesuits' home within two hours of arriving in the capital suggests that the unit may have been brought to San Salvador specifically for this purpose."[7]

❄   ❄   ❄

On November 13 at about 5:45 p.m. Father Ellacuría returned to the UCA campus after a working visit to Spain. When a soldier

---

[5] *Ibid.*, pp. 45-46.
[6] *Ibid.*, p. 46.
[7] *Ibid.*, p. 49.

recognized the university rector, he was allowed to proceed through the gate.

At 6:30 p.m. that same evening, one half hour after the start of curfew, some 135 troops surrounded the campus with the intention of searching the Jesuit residence and the Theological Reflection Center housed in the same building. "Two patrols, about 20 men, entered the campus by breaking the lock on the back gate.... Ellacuría introduced himself, and Lt. Espinoza Guerra addressed Fathers Segundo Montes and Ignacio Martín-Baró by name. Espinoza had been a student at the Jesuit high school, Externado San José, while Father Montes was its rector, although Montes did not recognize his former student. Ellacuría challenged the Army's right to examine the building without a search warrant and asked that the Minister of Defense be called."[8]

The officer justified the search by citing his orders and the state of siege imposed the previous day. "Ellacuría suggested that the men come back in daylight to search the rest of the UCA, but they did not return the next day. Father Montes later told colleagues that the troops were members of the Atlacatl Battalion.

"In contrast to earlier searches, no questions were asked and they did not seem interested in papers or books.... Salvadoran military officers have repeatedly said that neither weapons nor guerrillas were found during the search. Despite this fact, President Cristiani told reporters on July 12, 1990, that the soldiers did discover some arms. Further, a November 13, 1989, cable by U.S. military intelligence agents to the Defense Intelligence Agency, which was released to the

---

[8] *Ibid.*, p. 51.

Lawyers Committee[9] under the Freedom of Information Act, cited 'initial reports that the following equipment was captured by the Salvadoran Armed Forces...in the Jesuit priests' dormitory at the Catholic University."[10] Five rifles, three grenades, four pistols, and three radios are mentioned.

"Though clearly untrue, this report inexplicably surfaced in Senate offices in the days preceding the October 19, 1990, vote on a U.S. foreign assistance bill, which included a 50% reduction in military aid to El Salvador."

❄   ❄   ❄

On November 15 an Army officer posted in the UCA neighborhood commented to a Jesuit that there was going to be a lot of "movement" in the afternoon or evening.[11]   About 3 p.m. some 120-130 members of the Atlacatl entered Loyola Center, the Jesuit retreat house which was searched by Treasury Police on November 12. While searching the rooms, one soldier asked the housekeeper: "This also belongs to the UCA, right? Here they are planning the offensive." At about 7 p.m., after the fall of curfew, the men moved out and headed down toward the UCA campus.

---

[9] Author Martha Doggett works for the Lawyers Committee for Human Rights, which since 1978 has worked to promote international human rights and refugee law and legal procedures in the United States and abroad. The Committee has served as legal counsel to the Jesuits for this case.

[10] *Ibid.*, pp. 51-53.

[11] *Ibid.*, p. 53, citing a "Chronology of Events" written by the Central American Province of the Jesuits.

Before leaving Loyola, one officer said to someone present, "Yes, we're going to look for Ellacuría and all these Jesuits. We don't want foreigners. This has got to end." Another soldier warned the staff that "tonight there is going to be a big uproar around here. Stay inside and keep your heads down." Still another said that "we're going to look for Ellacuría, and if we find him we're going to be given a prize."[12]

In an attempt to establish when the decision was made to kill the Jesuits, "or perhaps when to implement longstanding contingency plans, attention has focused on a series of meetings held on November 15 at Joint Command headquarters. Top officers were known to be living at the military complex during the offensive, and President Cristiani reportedly spent several nights there as well.... According to Col. Ponce, some 24 top officers convened at about 7:30 p.m. on November 15 'to analyze the positions we had lost since November 11.... We analyzed what we needed to do to regain them. We understood that we needed to take stronger measures.'"[13]

Those who gathered that night included the Minister of Defense, the two vice ministers of defense, commanders of all the units in the metropolitan area, the commanders of special security zones, Security Force chiefs, the head of the military press office, COPREFA, and members of the Joint Command and its chief, Col. Ponce. "By their own account, top officers were in a state of near panic in the face of their inability to rout the FMLN.... Some observers believe that these officers have in retrospect exaggerated the severity of the FMLN challenge as well as their despair at the time in an attempt to rationalize the Jesuit murders and extensive aerial bombardment. Self-serving or

---

[12] *Ibid.*, p. 54.
[13] *Ibid.*, pp. 54-55, citing Lawyers Committee interview with Col. Ponce, February 14, 1990.

not, they describe an anguished mood that had gripped military ranks as the FMLN offensive entered its fifth day and showed no signs of abating."[14]

Officers present at the meeting have stated that the Jesuits were not mentioned in any way. President Cristiani told a group of visiting U.S. Jesuits on February 14, 1990, that he had not attended that meeting. Col. Ponce and others have said that the officers decided to step up the use of air power. According to the *Boston Sunday Globe* (February 4, 1990), "the meeting ended at about 10:30 p.m." and President Cristiani was "awakened and asked to sign an order authorizing the use of the air force and artillery, which he did." That was the night of the worst aerial bombardment.

Gen. Rafael Humberto Larios López, the Defense Minister in November 1989, stated "that after the meeting he called President Cristiani, who arrived at Joint Command headquarters at 11 p.m. and remained until about 2 a.m. on November 16. If accurate, this means that President Cristiani was present at Joint Command headquarters (with virtually the entire top military leadership of the country) while the Jesuit murder operation was in progress about one mile away." The Defense Minister's statement was corroborated by Cristiani in his September 7, 1990, testimony in the murder trial. He also said that the Jesuits were not mentioned during the meeting, during which he was asked to approve the use of heavier weaponry.

Cristiani also told the judge that at 12:30 a.m. on November 16 he and his personal secretary went to the command center at Joint Command headquarters to receive a briefing on the military situation in the capital. In the center at the time were "two or three North

---

[14] *Ibid.*, p. 55.

American military advisors," with whom the president said he did not converse.[15]

When was the order given to kill the Jesuits? Retired Col. Sigifredo Ochoa Pérez, a former senior Army field commander and now a leading member of the ARENA party, told the TV program *60 Minutes* on April 22, 1990, that a smaller group of officers gathered after the expanded High Command meeting on the evening of November 15. "At this meeting, Ochoa said, Col. Benavides was given a direct order to kill the Jesuits. Ochoa said: 'A group of commanders stayed behind. It seems each was responsible for a zone in San Salvador. They gave an order to kill leftists, just as Col. Benavides did. Benavides obeyed; it wasn't his decision.'"[16]

On May 3, 1990, a group of young military officers, who remained anonymous, expressed support for Ochoa's assertion.

Shortly after dawn on November 16, 1989, the daily meeting of the Salvadoran National Intelligence Directorate (DNI) began. The U.S. Central Intelligence Agency (CIA) "shared office space with the DNI, and CIA agents generally attended DNI meetings."[17] According to accounts in the U.S. press, "the officers present 'cheered and clapped' when Capt. Carlos Fernando Herrera Carranza announced that Fr. Ellacuría had died."[18] One source said the CIA was present at the meeting, while another said it was not.

---

[15] *Ibid.*, pp. 56-59.

[16] *Ibid.*, pp. 59-60. Doggett also noted (p. 132) that a source close to the Armed Forces told the Lawyers Committee that Col. Benavides turned to Gen. Bustillo and said, "I have the UCA in my sector, and Ellacuría is there."   Bustillo reportedly responded, "Well, then, you know what you have to do."

[17] *Ibid.*, p. 62.

[18] *Ibid.*, p. 63, citing *Boston Sunday Globe*, February 4, 1990, and *San Francisco Examiner*, February 5, 1990.

❄   ❄   ❄

According to the extrajudicial confessions of the defendants in the case, events unfolded in the following way. At 11 p.m. on November 15, Lt. Espinoza was ordered to report to Col. Benavides in the Military Academy. There he met Lt. Yusshy Mendoza Vallecillos, who repeated that the colonel wanted to see him and 2nd Lt. Guevara Cerritos. According to their accounts, Col. Benavides said: "This is a situation where it's them or us; we are going to begin with the ringleaders. Within our sector we have the university and Ellacuría is there." Turning to Lt. Espinoza, Benavides said: "You conducted the search and your people know the place. Use the same tactics as on the day of the search and eliminate him. And I want no witnesses. Lt. Mendoza will go with you as the man in charge of the operation so that there will be no problems."

The accounts of the two other lieutenants differ from this version on a few points. 2nd Lt. Guevara agrees with Espinoza but adds that Col. Benavides also said: "These are the intellectual authors who have directed the guerrillas for a long time." Lt. Mendoza asserts that when he entered the colonel's office, Lt. Espinoza was already there and Col. Benavides simply told him: "You are going to accompany Espinoza to carry out a mission. He already knows what it is."

❄   ❄   ❄

Lt. Espinoza says that he asked Lt. Mendoza for a bar of camouflage grease in order to paint his face. Espinoza had graduated from the Jesuit high school at a time when Fr. Segundo Montes was the rector. Espinoza asserts that Mendoza gave him the camouflage grease.

Just before leaving the Academy, Mendoza offered an AK-47 to any man who could use it. Oscar Mariano Amaya Grimaldi, an enlisted man from the Atlacatl Battalion, who would be charged with using it, does not remember which of the two lieutenants—Espinoza or Mendoza—gave it to him because the two were together. But he says that he was told by his commander, Espinoza, that they were going to kill "some delinquent terrorists who were inside the university UCA."[19]

Over 50 soldiers entered the campus, though not all of them played a direct role in the assassination. "The soldiers stated that they entered the UCA through the pedestrians' gate.... In front of the parking lot they feigned the first attack, damaging parked cars and launching at least one grenade. A night watchman who was sleeping in one of the buildings parallel to the parking lot later recounted that he heard two sentences: 'Don't go over there, there are only offices over there,' and 'now is the time to go kill the Jesuits.'"[20]

A small group would do the killing. "Only some of the members of this limited group were formally charged with the crime."[21] Some soldiers banged on the doors of the Jesuit house; others entered the lower floor of the building, the Theological Reflection Center, destroying and burning what they found. Five of the six Jesuits living in the house were brought out to the lawn in front of the residence: Ignacio Ellacuría, noted theologian and philosopher, rector of the university, and influential proponent of a negotiated settlement of the

---

[19] *Ibid.*, pp. 65-66.
[20] *Ibid.*, pp. 66-67.
[21] *Ibid.*, p. 67.

war; Amando López, former rector of the UCA in Managua, professor of theology; Ignacio Martín-Baró, professor of social psychology; Segundo Montes, director of the UCA's Institute for Human Rights; and Juan Ramón Moreno, professor of theology.

"Martín-Baró went with a soldier to open the gate leading to the chapel of Christ the Liberator. That is where the witness Lucía Barrera de Cerna saw five soldiers. There too, is probably where Martín-Baró said to a soldier: 'This is an injustice; you are scum.' Lucía Cerna heard this phrase perfectly.[22] It could be that Martín-Baró said these words when he saw that a soldier had pointed his rifle at Elba Ramos, a cook for the Jesuits, and her daughter Celina [who had taken refuge in the Theological Reflection Center]."[23]

The five priests were ordered to lie down on the lawn. Fr. Joaquín López y López (the only native Salvadoran among the six priests, director of Fe y Alegría, a network of schools for the poor) had managed to hide in another room. "At one point, just before the gunfire that killed the priests began, one neighbor says she heard a kind of rhythmic whispering, like a psalmody of a group in prayer."[24]

❄   ❄   ❄

"In his statement Antonio Avalos Vargas says that Lt. Espinoza, with Lt. Mendoza at his side, asked him, 'At what time are you going to

---

[22] Doggett explains that "the word used by Martín-Baró was *carroña,* meaning carrion or rotting flesh. While common in Spain, the word is generally not used in Central American Spanish."

[23] *Ibid.*, pp. 67-68.

[24] *Ibid.*, p. 68.

proceed?' The sub-sergeant declares that he understood this sentence 'as an order to eliminate the men who were lying face down.' He approached Private Amaya Grimaldi [known among his friends as Pilijay, a Nahuatl word meaning 'hangman'] and said to him: 'Let's proceed.'"[25]

Avalos killed Juan Ramón Moreno and Amando López. Pilijay shot Ellacuría, Martín-Baró, and Montes. "Espinoza and Mendoza remained 10 meters away, according to the testimony of one of the executioners.... While this was going on, Tomás Zarpate was 'providing security'—according to his own testimony—for Elba and Celina. On hearing the voice ordering 'now,' and the following shots, he 'also shot the two women' until he was sure they were dead, because 'they no longer groaned.'

"At this moment, when the shooting was over, Fr. López y López appeared in the door of the residence. The soldiers called him and Pilijay says that the priest responded: 'Don't kill me because I don't belong to any organization.' He then went back inside the house....

"According to Corporal Pérez Vásquez' narrative, 'just when Fr. López y López had entered a room a soldier shot him.' When Pérez Vásquez went in to inspect the scene, he 'felt Fr. López y López grab his feet. He moved back and shot him four times.'

"At the end of the shooting, the soldiers shot off a Bengal light, which was a signal to withdraw. When some did not move, they shot off another Bengal light. While leaving, Avalos Vargas—nicknamed 'Toad' and 'Satan' by his comrades—passed in front of the guest room where Elba and Celina were murdered and heard some people groaning. He surmised that some of the victims were merely wounded

---

[25] *Ibid.*

and would have to be shot again. According to his testimony, he 'lit a match, seeing that inside the room...were two women lying on the floor, embracing each other and moaning, so he ordered the soldier Sierra Ascencio to shoot them again.' Avalos Vargas testified that Jorge Alberto Sierra Ascencio, another member of the Atlacatl, 'shot off a round of about ten cartridges toward the bodies of these women until they stopped moaning.' Later, Sierra Ascencio realized that the investigation was focusing on his group and deserted."[26]

Amaya Grimaldi says he heard Lt. Espinoza Guerra order Corporal Cotta Hernández to drag the priests' bodies inside. Cotta "carried the body of Juan Ramón Moreno to Jon Sobrino's room and left him there. Lying next to him when his body was found was the book, *The Crucified God*, by the European theologian Jürgen Moltmann. Going outside the house, Cotta noticed that the other soldiers had left and he too left the UCA, leaving the other priests lying on the grass.

"The entire operation took about one hour. As the soldiers left, they feigned an attack on the Theological Reflection Center. It was part of the plan. The Joint Command's log contains the following entry: 'At 12:30 a.m. on November 16, delinquent terrorists launch grenades from the San Felipe sand ravine, on the southeast edge of the university, damaging the Theology Building, no casualties reported.' The Joint Command's report was only mistaken in the location from which the attack was launched and the hour. In fact, this record of the attack indicates it took place exactly two hours before it actually did.

"On the doors and walls of the lower floor of the Theological Reflection Center, the soldiers wrote the initials 'FMLN.' Exiting through the pedestrians' gate to the UCA, one of them scrawled 'The

---

[26] *Ibid.*, pp. 68-69.

FMLN executed the enemy spies. Victory or death, FMLN.' Handwriting analysts indicated that the handwriting of Guevara Cerritos and that of Avalos Vargas 'exhibits similar characteristics.' Several of the soldiers remembered having seen Guevara Cerritos write the message.

"By the time the priests had been killed, the Center had already been burned inside. Presumably Guevara Cerritos, who was not present at the scene of the assassination, directed the attack on the building. Later he set up an M-60 machine gun, brought from the Military Academy along with the AK-47, in front of the Center for Information and Documentation (CIDAI), the building opposite the Jesuit residence, and pointed it toward the Theological Center. Pilijay arrived in time to shoot off his anti-tank rocket, which exploded against the iron gate on the balcony of the priests' residence. He added his own shots to those of the M-60. Other soldiers also took shots at the building and one threw two M-79 grenades against it. Neither Cotta Hernández—who participated in the assassination by moving Juan Ramón Moreno's body—nor the sergeant nicknamed 'Savage' and his patrol, who shot up the building, nor those soldiers who entered the Theological Center and burned and destroyed its equipment, were charged with any crime. In his testimony Lt. Yusshy Mendoza added: 'An unidentified soldier took a light brown satchel,' he said. The bag, containing $5,000 in prize money which had been given to Ellacuría a few days earlier, has never reappeared."[27]

Upon returning to the Military Academy, Espinoza went to Col. Benavides' office "with the intention of confronting him, because he was angered by what had happened," according to his declaration. "'My

---

[27] *Ibid.*, pp. 69-70.

colonel, I did not like what was done,' he said. 'Calm down, don't worry, you have my support. Trust me,' Benavides replied.

"There were over 300 officers and enlisted men around the UCA and surrounding neighborhood that night, without even counting those who participated in the assassination. Apparently not one of them informed his superiors, or tried to initiate an investigation of what had happened at the UCA. The soldiers of the Atlacatl who participated in the assassination were sent to fight in the neighborhoods of Mejicanos and Zacamil at 6 a.m. on November 16, rejoining their own battalion. There they told soldiers of the First Brigade what they had done. Between 2 and 3 p.m. this same day, Archbishop Rivera y Damas and Auxiliary Bishop Rosa Chávez heard a voice over a megaphone on a military sound truck saying, 'Ellacuría and Martín-Baró have fallen; we're going to continue killing Communists.' Minutes later, the same voice on the same microphone said, 'Surrender. We belong to the First Brigade.' Despite the public denunciation by Rosa Chávez and others, this lead was never investigated."[28]

On the day of the martyrs' funeral, Archbishop Rivera y Damas stated publicly that all indications were that the military had perpetrated the crime.

❄   ❄   ❄

Fr. José María Tojeira, Jesuit Provincial of Central America, preached at the funeral on November 19:

---

[28] *Ibid.*, p. 71.

"'I have come to give testimony to the truth' (John 18:37). I believe that these words of Jesus define and clarify the death of our brother Jesuits. Everything about their lives was characterized by an ardent search for truth. They sought the truth about God and tried to make that truth accessible to people. They sought the truth about humanity, and they devoted themselves to discovering and helping the world to see the seeds of the Risen One present in the suffering and solidarity of the poor. They sought the truth about the world and about the reality of this little part of the world called El Salvador, and they sought to move this reality forward on the road of justice, brotherhood and sisterhood, dialogue, and toward an open society where the poor would be able to speak their word and maintain their dignity.

"Because they sought the truth and proclaimed that part of the truth they were finding, they were assassinated, like so many others in El Salvador, like Archbishop Romero. And they were killed because that truth helped the poor. That truth, which came out of their work in the university, out of their personal testimony and their prophetic denunciation, was opening people's awareness and conscience, favoring the consciousness-raising and organization of the poor, and helping to foresee a future of real brotherhood and sisterhood in deeds and not only in words. They looked toward a future without these rivers of blood unjustly spilt, without hunger and misery, without hearts ripped asunder by the hatred, fear, mistrust, and violence which are due to the fact that very few have too much and too many have nothing.

"Lovers of utopia, they were realists and knew how to take the small steps that were necessary. They never settled for compromise. They knew how to make demands and speak the truth even in the midst of a civil war which polarizes and divides and often hides basic elements of reality. They knew how to defend life; they knew that peace must be based on the rights of the poor; and they spoke with an academic rigor which made the light of truth clearer and even more brilliant.

"Their testimony to the truth has now been sealed with blood in their death. This is the last word which our brothers have spoken, as a community, as martyrs. It has united them to the immense chorus of so many Salvadorans assassinated because of their hunger and thirst for justice. The martyrs are at the same time seed, flower, and fruit. Their death, in the midst of the blood of the people, has joined them to that suffering face of the Lord Jesus which is seen today in Latin America in the faces of the marginated of our cities, the peasants without land, the indigenous people without a voice, the children without hope, the elderly who receive kindness from no one, the persecuted and those killed because they worked so that the gospel would become life in our people. These faces have been destroyed, without a doubt, by the selfishness of a certain few, by the sin of all, by the brutality of those who believe that death is the solution for human problems. All these faces destroyed are symbolically represented by the faces of our brothers destroyed by automatic-weapons fire.

"'My Kingdom is not of this world,' said Jesus, joining these words to his commitment to the truth. Our brothers worked for that Kingdom which is not built by the selfishness predominant in this world, in which three fourths of the population goes hungry. They did not seek honor, glory, position, but simply to serve. They did not seek their own interests, but they loved the suffering people of El Salvador with all their heart, and they put their own word and life at the service of that people.

"Can this world dominated by selfishness destroy the dynamism of the Kingdom? Can the testimony of the truth be killed? Our faith in the Risen Lord tells us no. And, if you will pardon this personal testimony, my own experience, short as it is, as provincial of the Society of Jesus in Central America confirms for me that nothing and no one can destroy the testimony of the truth. That truth is not ours but is built with the destroyed body and the shed blood of Jesus Christ, united with the blood and the destroyed bodies of those to whom the Lord gives the grace to be witnesses to the truth.

"I can say today with pride that while the same hatred which killed Archbishop Romero was cutting down the lives of our companions, our young Jesuit seminarians were working in the provisional refugee shelters of the archdiocese, accompanying our brothers and sisters from the neighborhoods which have been hit especially hard by this war, gathering up the dead and dying of both sides in the midst of the madness of a struggle without any truce. They were protecting children and accompanying those fleeing from the bullets of the combat zones, consoling those who were losing their loved ones, staying at the side of the poor. They have not killed the Society of Jesus! They have not killed the José Simeon Canas University [Central American University]. [At this point everyone in the auditorium stood and applauded for about two minutes.]

"The testimony of the truth continues. Love is stronger than death. Our brothers have worthy successors in the Society of Jesus and among the lay people of the UCA [Central American University], ready to serve in the Church, in the University, in El Salvador, always at the side of the poor and united in courage and commitment to Archbishop Romero, to so many good priests who have gone before us with their example, to so many unknown lay persons, witnesses with their love and blood.

"May so much testimony proclaimed in blood become an urgent cry for peace. No to death! No to war! No to injustice! Yes to the love of the Beatitudes transforming the structures of human relations! Yes to the constant testimony, in life and word, of the truth about God, about human beings, and about the world in which we live!

"There is no Christian witness to the truth without Eucharist. Our companions Elba Ramos, Celina, Segundo Montes, Ellacuría, Joaquin López, Amando, Juan Ramón Moreno, and Ignacio Martín-Baró are now united to the Lord in death and in the spirit. May our Eucharist become an intimate communion and commitment in the Body and the Blood of the Lord Jesus in whom our brothers now live."

❄   ❄   ❄

On December 12, Fr. Tojeira issued a "public communique of the Society of Jesus" in which he stated: "Since the assassination we have been gathering data from various witnesses, and this information continues to point toward elements of the Armed Forces. At first we were speaking of the curfew, the duration of the attack and the fact that it was done with impunity, and the heavy militarization of the area; now there is additional data from new witnesses.

"Among other things, which point toward the same conclusion, there is the use of flares during the time of the crime, the fact that the perpetrators of the crime spent at least 3 hours on the university grounds and behaved like persons who know they are protected....

"While we are not saying that the investigative process is totally in doubt, we do want to make clear for public opinion a series of occurrences which we consider irregular. While the Society of Jesus has received an excellent report from Tutela Legal (the human rights office of the archdiocese), we have received very little information about the investigation from those who are carrying it out. At times we have even been deceived with regard to certain aspects of the investigation. The clearest instance of this is the way in which the witness, Lucía Barrera de Cerna, has been manipulated in the U.S."

This witness (an employee of the UCA) and her husband were staying on campus in a house very close to the scene of the crime. She testified that she saw five men in military garb on the grounds of the Jesuit residence and that she heard Fr. Ignacio Martín-Baró say to them: "This is an injustice; you are scum." With the assistance of Spanish and French diplomats, the couple were flown to Miami; Jesuits in El Salvador had arranged for U.S. Jesuits to take them under their care and protection.

At his own insistence, a U.S. embassy official also accompanied the couple to Miami; upon arrival they were taken to a hotel where they were held by the FBI for a week of incommunicado questioning. The interrogation, in which Salvadoran Lt. Col. Manuel Antonio Rivas Mejía (chief of the Special Investigative Unit) participated, was insulting and threatening. "Intimidated and wishing to end the ordeal, Mrs. Cerna recanted after four days in FBI custody, saying she had seen no soldiers on the campus on the murder night. 'They pressured me until I couldn't stand it any more,' she told the Lawyers Committee on December 3 when she was finally released to the Jesuits. She repeatedly failed lie detector tests on her revised story."[29]

U.S. officials leaked the story to the press, saying Mrs. Cerna admitted having lied. President Cristiani gave the same message publicly. In response, an angry Archbishop Rivera y Damas said Mrs.

---

[29] *Ibid.*, pp. 218-219.

Cerna had been subjected to "aggressive and violent" interrogations, and continued: "Instead of being protected, as officials in the U.S. embassy in El Salvador had promised, she was subjected...to a veritable brainwashing and to the blackmail that she would be deported if she was not telling the truth." U.S. Ambassador Walker said that the archbishop was misinformed.

The treatment Mrs. Cerna received was not the kind which would encourage others to come forth with information. In his December 12 statement, Fr. Tojeira continued: "In effect, the U.S. embassy made a commitment to accompany the witness to Miami and to hand her over there to priests of the Society of Jesus. That was also what the witness wanted. Instead, she was handed over to U.S. police agents for eight days under the pretext of watching out for her security and with no attention to the wishes which had been expressed here.

"The interrogation sessions were excessively long, without anyone she could trust being present who could advise her how to react to pressures she was receiving." She was in a very tense emotional state. "The investigative methods were also abusive, unjust, and improper: the witness was subjected to a lie-detector test six times while in a state of exhaustion, nervousness, and insecurity.

"During questioning the American agents pressured the witness on various occasions to give the names of the priests who supposedly had pressured her to speak. After having seen how six priests had been assassinated, this kind of question increased the witness's nervousness and led her into contradictions. The same could be said of the veiled threat the witness received that she could be returned to El Salvador if her statements did not satisfy the demands of her interrogators. During at least part of the interrogation a representative of the Salvadoran

Special Investigative Unit was present." The fact that the representative was a military official was even more intimidating.[30]

❄   ❄   ❄

A January 3, 1990, statement by U.S. Maj. Eric Buckland, the senior U.S. military advisor attached to C-5 (Psychological Operations) at the Joint Command, "unleashed a sequence of events culminating in President Cristiani's January 7, 1990, announcement that members of the Armed Forces were responsible for the murders.... It was 10 months after the murders that Buckland first appeared before Salvadoran judicial authorities and 11 months before the second portion of his testimony was leaked out of Washington.... It is impossible to know with hindsight what turn the investigation might have taken had the court been aware of the full scope of his account in January 1990.

"About December 20, 1989, Col. Carlos Armando Avilés Buitrago, the C-5 chief, told Maj. Buckland that the Atlacatl commando unit, working out of the Military Academy, committed the killings at the UCA on the orders of Col. Guillermo Alfredo Benavides Moreno. Avilés said he had received this information from Col. Iván López y López, who in turn had been briefed by Lt. Col. Manuel Antonio Rivas Mejía, chief of the Special Investigative Unit (SIU--a U.S.-trained and financed criminal investigatory body whose agents are members of the Security Forces).

---

[30] The United Nations Truth Commission later found Lt. Col. Rivas guilty of involvement in the coverup.

"The chain of information was thus as follows: Benavides→Rivas Mejía→López y López→Avilés →Buckland. In a one-page statement written in San Salvador on January 3, 1990, Buckland said:

> Col. López y López had told [Avilés] that Lt. Col. Rivas had told him Col. Benavides had admitted his responsibility in the slayings of the Jesuits. Again— when the investigation of the killings had started Col. Benavides had approached Lt. Col. Rivas and said something to the effect of 'I did it. What can you do to help me?' According to Col. Avilés, Lt. Col. Rivas was scared and did not know what to do. As a result, the investigation slowed and eventually Col. López y López went to talk to Lt. Col. Rivas. During the conversation Lt. Col. Rivas told Col. López y López about Col. Benavides' comments.[31]

"Avilés had emphasized that Buckland was only to make use of this information on a 'Break in Case of Emergency' basis [*i.e.*, in case the investigation did not unfold properly or if Avilés should be killed].[32] When asked if Col. Ponce knew, Avilés said he 'believed that he did, but wasn't sure. [Avilés] did not feel that it was his place to tell him,' Buckland said in his written account of the conversation.... In retrospect, Buckland told his superiors that he assumed that the Salvadoran investigation would proceed apace and that arrests were imminent...."

---

[31] *Ibid.*, pp. 221-222.
[32] *Ibid.* Sworn statement of Maj. Eric Warren Buckland to the FBI, January 11, 1990, Washington, D.C.

Several days after the first conversation with Avilés, Buckland said (in his court testimony in September, 1990), he raised the issue again with the Salvadoran colonel and asked if Col. Ponce knew about Benavides' role. Buckland remembered that Avilés raised his hands and asked rhetorically, "What if the superiors ordered the assassination of the Jesuits?" After this exchange, Buckland told Judge Zamora, he "realized he had a problem because he was no longer sure what was going on."[33]

On January 2, 1990, Buckland mentioned the conversation to his immediate superior, Lt. Col. William C. Hunter, senior U.S. advisor to the Joint Command.... Hunter immediately went to the U.S. embassy and briefed Col. Milton Menjívar, the MilGroup commander, who went to Joint Command headquarters to give the story to Col. Ponce. Asked what he knew about the matter, Ponce said, 'I haven't the slightest idea.' In August 1991, Col. Menjívar recalled that 'first of all, Ponce seemed surprised, then he was sort of disappointed and then outraged. He didn't believe—he wanted to know where the information came from.'[34]

When Col. Avilés was called to Col. Ponce's office, he arrived about an hour later and denied his role in the affair. After Buckland joined the meeting, accompanied by Hunter, Avilés repeated his denial.[35] Col. López y López also denied everything.

Early the next day, January 3, 1990, Col. Menjívar met with members of the Salvadoran High Command. Menjívar repeated the story to the Defense Minister, the two Vice Ministers of Defense, the

---

[33] *Ibid.*, p. 168.
[34] Deposition of Col. Milton Menjívar, August 7, 1991, in re Letters Rogatory from the Fourth Criminal Court Judge of San Salvador, El Salvador.
[35] Doggett, *op. cit.*, pp. 222-224.

Deputy Chief of Staff, and Col. Ponce. A source with knowledge of what transpired at the meeting told the Lawyers Committee: "Their faces were as white as sheets. They were nervous about how much more [the Americans] knew. All five were scared." Col. Montano [one of the Vice Ministers of Defense] was the first to respond: "There may be some truth to what you are saying," he reportedly told the U.S. officer.

That morning, Buckland prepared a one-page statement regarding what he knew and how. In an affidavit of January 6, sent to the FBI in Washington, Buckland indicated for the first time that he had had prior knowledge that a group of Salvadoran officers planned to kill some Jesuits, including Fr. Ellacuría. On January 12 in a videotape for the FBI Buckland presented the most complete account of his "prior knowledge" of the crime.

Buckland told the FBI that at some point in late October or early November 1989, Col. Avilés asked Buckland to go with Avilés to the Military Academy. "During their visit Avilés met with Col. Benavides for about 15 minutes. Avilés told Buckland that Col. Ponce had sent him there to 'solve a problem with Col. Benavides.' After meeting with Benavides, Avilés told Buckland that Benavides 'wanted to do something about the priests and things coming out of the UCA. Benavides told Avilés that Ella Coria [sic] was a problem.' In his affidavit Buckland says 'Avilés told me they wanted to handle it in the old way by killing some of the priests.'"[36]

As to why he had done nothing to prevent the killings, Buckland said: "I felt unconcerned that it would happen because other people were talking along those lines and I didn't feel that the El Salvadoran Armed Forces would do something about it. Also because Chief of

---

[36] *Ibid.*, p. 225.

Staff Ponce assigned a senior Colonel (Avilés) to address the problem I felt that if there was any validity to this talk it would not happen."

A week later, Buckland officially recanted the prior knowledge story to the FBI at Ft. Bragg, North Carolina. Buckland's January 11 affidavit and the videotape were given to Richard Chidester, legal officer at the embassy, by the FBI on January 13, 1990. Embassy officials and ranking State Department officials in Washington who were briefed by the FBI on the contents of the statements decided not to share this information with the public or with the court.[37]

"While the gist of Buckland's story as well as his role in late December 1989 and early January 1990 had appeared in both the Salvadoran and U.S. press,[38] the account was first laid out in full in the *Interim Report* published by the Moakley task force on April 30, 1990. The congressional task force respected the wishes of the Pentagon by not publishing Maj. Buckland's name, referring simply to 'an American major.'[39]

"The inappropriateness of the embassy's handling of Buckland is evidenced by the fact that it was not until May 29, 1990—one month after the story appeared in the Moakley report—that Judge Zamora felt he had the backing even to request a copy of Buckland's statement. Neither the embassy nor military authorities had seen fit to submit a copy of the document to the court."[40]   It was not until June 6, 1990, that

---

[37] *Ibid.*, p. 226.

[38] *Miami Herald*, January 16, 1990; *New York Times*, January 14, 1990.

[39] "The Report found that the 'timing of events is such that it is not clear whether the case ever would have been broken if the American Major did not come forward'(Doggett, p. 232)."   The *Miami Herald* quoted a diplomatic source to the same effect.

[40] Doggett, pp. 227-228.

the document was added to the court record. On July 18 the Foreign Ministry asked that Buckland appear before the judge. He appeared over two months later, on September 28, 1990. The State Department, in consultation with the Pentagon, set the conditions for Buckland's appearance. He was not to reveal the existence of the prior knowledge story, and there were to be no questions regarding what happened after January 6, 1990.

Congressman Moakley issued a statement on October 18, 1990 about the additional Buckland testimony given to the FBI on January 10, 11, 12, and 18. Moakley said that "if the information is accurate, Salvadoran military authorities should have considered Col. Benavides the prime suspect immediately after the murders took place."[41]

Doggett notes several parallels between the embassy's handling of the Cerna and the Buckland testimonies. "As with Mrs. Cerna, U.S. diplomats took steps which had the effect of cordoning off and discrediting information implicating the Salvadoran Armed Forces. In Buckland's case, they did so even when the source was an embassy colleague. The actions of the embassy staff served to undermine any follow-up investigative efforts. Legal officer Richard Chidester immediately phoned Lt. Col. Rivas and told him the story, despite the fact that Rivas himself was implicated in the cover-up....

"Major Buckland himself came under attack, and, like Mrs. Cerna, was treated as a hostile witness.... Several U.S. officials referred to Buckland as 'unstable' and an 'emotional basket case.' Perhaps most remarkable is that U.S. officials failed to examine the role of the Special Investigative Unit (SIU), whose integrity was called into question by Buckland's testimony. If Col. Benavides in fact confessed to Lt. Col.

---

[41] *Ibid.*, p. 228

Rivas [of the SIU], who failed to act on the information, Rivas himself was criminally liable for his role in the coverup."[42]

On January 5, 1990, Gen. Larios appointed a military Honor Commission to examine the evidence, and six of the future murder defendants were arrested. On January 7, President Cristiani, flanked by the Army High Command, announced on Salvadoran television that "elements of the Armed Forces" were responsible for the Jesuit killings. On January 8 future defendants Lt. Mendoza and Col. Benavides were detained. On January 12 the Honor Commission delivered its report to Cristiani, naming nine suspects and excluding the possibility that other military men were involved. On the following day, Cristiani publicly named the nine defendants. One had reportedly fled in late December.[43]

In March 1990 Judge Zamora requested the logbooks of entries and exits to the Military Academy during the month of November 1989 as well as the names of guards on duty the night of November 15-16, 1989. Later that month the court was told that the logbook had been "misplaced." In May Lt. Col. Rivas reported that the logbooks had been burned on the orders of interim Deputy Academy Director Lt. Col. Hernández, who was later charged with and convicted of destruction of evidence. As for the guards on duty the night of the murders, the first list sent to the judge proved to be mistaken; when those who indeed were on duty that night finally testified, they had nothing to say.

On July 12, 1990, President Cristiani admitted publicly for the first time that he authorized the search of the UCA on November 13, 1989, and alleged erroneously that weapons were found in the Jesuit residence.

---

[42] *Ibid.*, pp. 232-233.
[43] *Ibid.*, pp. 284-285.

The First Anniversary—
"They Are Not Here"

The Jesuit provincial's message to the relatives of the martyred Jesuits in El Salvador on the first anniversary of the massacre was clear and consoling: "They are not here," he said, echoing the words at the tomb of the risen Jesus. They are now "giving life in all parts of the world," he explained, "not just in El Salvador." Their presence and witness is felt far beyond their university campus and far beyond the small country for whose people they gave their lives, he said during a Mass with the relatives. Their written and spoken words are being published widely, impacting much more strikingly than before November 16, 1989.

Testimony of this was given by visitors from many countries; and within El Salvador people kept telling how the martyrs are still present, walking with them, giving them courage and hope. In one Christian base community people spoke of the fear which had kept them from helping the victims of the aerial bombing, the government's response to the urban guerrilla activity initiated on November 11, 1989; but the martyrdom of the Jesuits gave them new strength and they took the risks. They also found help in community and in the Word of God to control their fear. (Some of the new communities of returned refugees are named after the Jesuits.)

In his homily during a Mass commemorating the anniversary, the provincial superior of the Jesuits in Central America emphasized that his six brothers in the order are not in the tombs made for them in the wall of the campus chapel, a site which their relatives were visiting and decorating for the first time. He noted that they are giving courage to the whole people of God but suggested that their power was being felt especially by bishops and priests, who were speaking out clearly against the atrocity, the cover-up and stalling which ensued, and the general situation of institutionalized violence.

Visual messages in the chapel are also compelling. Along the back wall are a series of large drawings of tortured and mangled bodies, representing the present way of the Cross. Looking to the front, one meditates on various multi-colored paintings. In one, the lower panel shows a coffin with skull and bones inside and with two rifles pointing at it from either side. Below the guns are large bills in the amount of one million, without dollar signs but suggesting the U.S. government as the donor (which it clearly is). The panels above depict resurrection scenes.

The offertory hymn was the prayer of St. Ignatius Loyola, the 16th-century founder of the Jesuits: "Take, Lord, and receive all my liberty, my memory, my understanding, and my entire will, all that I have and possess. You have given all to me. To you, O Lord, I return it. All is yours, dispose of it wholly according to your will. Give me your love and your grace, for this is sufficient for me." Ignatius suggested that retreatants following his Spiritual Exercises make this prayer their own; the slain Jesuits had meditated often on this prayer, and on what their founder pointed out just before presenting the prayer: "Love ought to manifest itself in deeds rather than in words."

❄   ❄   ❄

At the next day's Mass celebrated in the large auditorium, one of the offertory gifts brought up to the altar was a copy of *The Crucified God* by Jürgen Moltmann, dark red with the blood of Juan Ramón Moreno. The book, which had been on Jon Sobrino's bookshelf, fell into the blood after Juan Ramón's body was brought into the house and thrown on the floor of Jon's room.

❄   ❄   ❄

At 2 a.m. on November 16, 1990, exactly one year after the killings, Mass was celebrated as part of an all-night vigil. That afternoon, over 4,000 people, including fourteen bishops (with several from the United States) and 200 priests, participated in the outdoor Mass on campus. Some of the readings were done, somewhat falteringly but movingly, by newly literate peasants whose love for the martyrs came through clearly to the assembly. Jars containing blood-soaked earth from the yard where the Jesuits were slaughtered were presented to their relatives, who brought them to the center of the altar. At that moment I remembered with gratitude how Phil Berrigan and I had put some of that same blood-soaked earth, mingled with our own blood, on the front gate of the White House in January 1990, while friends held large poster-size pictures of the bodies for all to see and then lay down on the sidewalk, representing thousands of victims of U.S.-sponsored repression. (See Appendix One.)

❊   ❊   ❊

During the following days many visitors went to the parishes where the Jesuits had worked as pastors on weekends. They had fallen in love with the people, and the people with them. In Jayaque the people remembered clearly the last biblical text which Ignacio ("Nacho") Martín-Baró preached on: Zaccheus's conversion to justice (Luke 19:1-10). They also remembered how, just after the killings, repression in the village escalated, with government troops entering the church and arresting a parish leader and his daughter.

"Nacho" used his expertise in social psychology to analyze society, making his findings public in El Salvador and internationally. "There is nothing more subversive, more contrary to the official discourse, than Salvadoran reality itself," he stated in a paper he would have delivered at a meeting of the Latin American Studies Association in Miami in December, 1989.

Lutheran pastor William Dexheimer, who was working in El Salvador in 1989, has written: "To the poor campesinos and slumdwellers of the rural and urban parishes he served part-time during his years in El Salvador, he was simply 'Padre Nacho' or sometimes, with deep affection, 'Papa Nacho.' He could speak the language of the poor; they laughed at his jokes and funny songs. He played a couple of *ranchera* style folk songs that delighted the people, bellowing out the lyrics in his deep rich voice.

"His voice will be dearly missed, along with those of his brother Jesuits. Their presence in the country—their writings, their polls, the countless interviews on television they did—were a major force behind the movement towards a peaceful, negotiated solution to the conflict in El Salvador. They were killed by men who do not want a peaceful solution."

Dexheimer presented some remarks made by 'Nacho" in a 1984 conversation:

"As long as the United States wants to keep complete hegemony, no solution is possible. It is in your best interest to let Latin American countries try different paths."

"People in the United States say Latin Americans are lazy, but when we try to change anything, they intervene and stomp on us."

"I feel the people crying for justice. It gives me hope. I have learned more from these poor people than in all my years of studies."

"Have you forgotten Vietnam already? Anything happens and you immediately see RED! Poor people here are fighting for their most basic human rights, and they are being crushed in the name of God and Western Civilization."

"When those in power in your country are supporting the bombing of children in El Salvador, you all must bear responsibility for that. Remember: the *silent* majority just might be the *criminal* majority."

"In the end the problem is not the national security of the United States. The problem is poverty in the Third World."

In an introduction to his 1983 book, *Acción e Ideología*, "Nacho" stated: "As a social scientist, I do not find it easy to live within such a convulsive process (as that of El Salvador). The most obvious difficulty concerns the risking of one's life when one attempts to shed light on the problems that are at the root of the conflict, or when one looks for a solution. People are not interested in understanding reality, even when that reality is so obvious, so clear, when the very act of naming it constitutes a 'subversive' act....

"Our ultimate objective consists in articulating the perspective of the 'condemned of the earth' of Central America, in our work in social psychology both as science and as praxis. Because of this, the definitive criterion for judging the value of this work cannot be defined in terms of academic rigor or its coherence in some abstract way, but rather by looking at its effective contribution, however modest it may be, to the process of liberation of the people of Central America."[44]

❄   ❄   ❄

Riding out to the Tierra Virgen neighborhood where Amando López had served, I noticed a message proclaimed on a large sign at the entrance to Salvadoran Air Force headquarters: "Parachutists never die; they rise up to regroup in heaven." Such crude manipulation of Christian faith stood in contrast to the message given at the start of a large procession in Tierra Virgen. A parish worker said over the portable loudspeakers: "We have good news." I expected her to refer to the visitors or to the completion of some new parish building or a

---

[44] Bill Dexheimer, "Reflections on the Ministry of Papa Nacho," 1991.

break-through in the peace talks. "Padre Amando and the others have risen and are with us, giving us strength and courage."

Youngsters recalled one of Amando's expressions designed to get them to ask questions, speak out, participate: "Don't be benches." People here, like those in Jayaque, remembered and found great significance in the last bible passage their martyr had recommended to them for their group study a week before he was killed: Isaiah 43:1-7. His message to them, and to himself, was that of God: "Be not afraid, I am with you." Raging seas and burning coals, and death itself, cannot destroy the faithfulness of the prophet. (This text is the basis for the beautiful "Be Not Afraid" recorded by the St. Louis Jesuits.)

In the United States the first anniversary was observed with a variety of religious services and direct-action protests. On November 16 Maryknoll Father Roy Bourgeois, Charles Liteky (a former Army chaplain who won the Medal of Honor in Vietnam), and the latter's brother Patrick (who had trained at Ft. Benning) entered the post [Ft. Benning], placed a white cross with photos of the eight martyrs at the entrance to the School of the Americas, and poured blood in one of the school's main halls. "We wanted to impress on our country," wrote Fr. Bourgeois later from prison, "that we cannot wash our hands of the blood of innocent people killed in El Salvador by soldiers trained in the United States."[45] They had mixed their blood with the blood-stained soil from the site where the Jesuits had been killed. The action

---

[45] "Thoughts from an Imprisoned Priest: Despite Bloody History, U.S. Still Trains Latin Soldiers," by Fr. Roy Bourgeois, MM, *Miami Herald*, June 6, 1992.

had been preceded by a 35-day water-only fast at the entrance to the base conducted by ten people, including Vietnam veterans, Salvadorans, a teacher, and members of the clergy (including Bourgeois).

The priest, who had served in the Navy in the Vietnam War before entering the seminary, was sentenced to 16 months in federal prison, while each of the Litekys was sentenced to 6 months. The deaths of two friends—Maura Clarke and Ita Ford—"made me confront what was happening in El Salvador," Bourgeois wrote. "Five of the nine soldiers arrested" for the slaying of the eight at the UCA in 1989 "had been trained at Ft. Benning's Army School of the Americas." In addition, the school's "distinguished graduates" include Gen. Manuel Noriega, Gen. Hugo Banzer Suarez (Bolivian dictator 1971-1978), Gen. Hector Gramajo (retired Guatemalan defense minister),[46] and Maj. Joseph-Michel Francois (Haitian chief of police who played a key role in the September 1991 coup that ousted President Aristide).

Fr. Bourgeois had made his first visit to Ft. Benning in 1983. With two friends, he entered the grounds dressed as an Army officer and climbed a tree just outside the barracks where a large contingent of Salvadoran military trainees were housed. Bourgeois turned on a boom box so the cadets could hear a recording of Archbishop Romero's 1980 sermon in which he ordered troops to stop killing their own people. The priest was sentenced to eighteen months in prison by the same federal judge who had commuted the sentence of Lt. William Calley, Jr., who massacred Vietnamese civilians at My Lai.

---

[46] See Appendix One.

CHAPTER 2

The Second Anniversary

"You must shine among them like
stars lighting up the sky, as you
offer them the message of life"
(Philippians 2:15).

The sisters killed in El Salvador in 1980 and the Jesuits killed there in 1989 must have been on flights like this, I thought to myself, as my flight from Miami approached the San Salvador airport in November, 1991. They were returning to their work with the poor and with the people's struggles for liberation and dignity.

Also, I mused, U.S. government officials have traveled this route innumerable times, bringing support for a government which has never served the poor majority and for a military system which has repressed the people and slaughtered thousands (including a bishop, sisters, and priests) when they struggle for their rights.

Stopping U.S. military aid was the objective of a one-week "Fast and Prayer against Military Aid" in September in Ciudad Segundo Montes, one of the communities of returned refugees. Eighty people from various communities participated, specifically to protest military actions which had destroyed their crops and threatened their lives and liberty.

Participants said that in the fast they had experienced their unity with one another and with God, "the God of Life who gives us strength and nourishes our faith and hope." Lucila Campos, whose whole family took part in the fast against military aid, said: "As poor people, we are marginated, tortured and exploited like animals; they have treated us like dogs ever since the war began. Now, because of the Air Force bombing raids, the children are afraid to go to school; and when soldiers pass by the children run in fright, since they know that anyone who gets captured is as good as dead."

In a letter to the U.S. Congress, the fasters said: "We do not understand how you can be so concerned about having peace among the more powerful countries, almost all in the northern part of the globe, while at the same time you keep promoting and participating in wars in countries like ours.

"Furthermore, you sometimes take economic, political, or military sanctions against countries in order to save freedom, as you put it." The letter mentioned U.S. intervention against Iraq. "But you do not take any serious sanctions against armies and governments like ours which constantly impede the exercise of freedom, justice, and human rights."

They added that a cutoff of military aid would assist the stalled negotiations between the FMLN and the government and would contribute to clarifying the Jesuit case and others. The dollars "could promote true development and reconstruction, especially if they were channeled through the people's organizations."[1]

---

[1] *Mártires de El Salvador (boletín de las Comunidades Eclesiales de Base de El Salvador)*, Sept-Oct 1991.

❄   ❄   ❄

On the eve of the second anniversary, hundreds of people took part in a candlelight procession through the neighborhood of the university. Walking alongside me, a young sister told me that there were "ears" (snitches) around. On the way we stopped at various stations where each of the eight martyrs was remembered. At one of these, a text was read which seems to have special meaning in Latin America these days: "We who have this spiritual treasure are like common clay pots, in order to show that the supreme power belongs to God, not to us. We are often troubled, but not crushed; sometimes in doubt, but never in despair; there are many enemies, but we are never without a friend; and though badly hurt at times, we are not destroyed. At all times we carry in our mortal bodies the death of Jesus, so that his life also may be seen in our bodies" (2 Cor 4:7-10). (Part of this text appears on the masthead of *Carta a las Iglesias*, a publication of the UCA.)

Shortly after 1 a.m. (November 16), Mass began with a Spanish version of "We Shall Overcome." The Gospel text from Luke proclaimed the Beatitudes in all their stark splendor. The occasion underlined the final verses: "Happy are you when people hate you, reject you, insult you, and say that you are evil, all because of the Son of Man!...Their ancestors did the very same things to the prophets" (Luke 6:22-23).

The consecration took place at 2 a.m., the likely moment of the martyrs' shedding of blood and breaking of their bodies. "Do this in memory of me." Do what? Would the priest concelebrants pronouncing those words, as the six of the UCA had so often, some day have to give literal expression to them in martyrdom? How many others in that

Eucharist would have to give that ultimate expression of love? Short of that, how can we live and work in such ways that we live out that self-giving?

At an earlier Mass on the 15th in the packed auditorium, each department had offered a symbol expressing its particular way of contributing to the university's mission to analyze and change society; e.g., philosophy said it would strive to unmask the social and cultural myths which cover over and sometimes rationalize injustice and oppression. The Mass also celebrated some of the fruits of the blood shed in martyrdom: *e.g.*, a new commitment by the university to public health, the launching of a new radio station. Fr. Francisco Estrada, the rector of the university, later stated that the "peasants and workers are the horizon, the compass which orientates our university work," noting that professors are evaluated not only on their technical expertise but also on their ability to relate their knowledge to the "national reality which consists mainly of peasants and workers."

On the 15th a special Mass had also been celebrated at the University of Innsbruck in Austria, where Ellacuría and Montes had studied theology (under Karl Rahner, among others) and had been ordained. A special plaque commemorating these two martyred alumni was unveiled. It is located on a monument which already had another plaque, this one in memory of Christoph Probst, a medical student and member of the resistance group "the White Rose," who was executed by the Nazis in 1943.[2]

❄   ❄   ❄

---

[2] *Carta a las Iglesias*, December 1-15, 1991.

The principal Mass of the anniversary began at 11 a.m. on November 16, with Archbishop Rivera y Damas presiding, about 80 priests concelebrating, and 1,000 people participating. U.S. Ambassador William Walker attended, as he had the funeral and the first anniversary. His presence intensified my feeling of responsibility as a U.S. citizen for the institutionalized violence done to the Salvadoran people with the support of our government. I felt I was addressing the Salvadorans as we said: "I confess to almighty God and to you, my brothers and sisters...."

The first reading, which Central American provincial Fr. José María Tojeira focused on in his homily, presented the words of Paul: "Do everything without complaining or arguing, so that you may be innocent and pure as God's perfect children, who live in a world of corrupt and sinful people. You must shine among them like stars lighting up the sky, as you offer them the message of life.... Perhaps my life's blood is to be poured out like an offering on the sacrifice that your faith offers to God. If that is so, I am glad and share my joy with you all" (Philippians 2:14-17).

"Our brothers," the provincial began, "continue to shine like stars in the midst of this El Salvador which remains at war, against the will of the majority. They shine in the positive signs now to be seen in our society: in the courage of those who today are speaking out more clearly, in the good will of those who are seeking negotiated solutions to the conflict, in the promise and hope of a peace built on justice.

"Can there be any doubt that many of the advances in the negotiations have been forced to come about because of the world-wide indignation sparked by the assassination of our eight brothers and sisters of the UCA?" (During the Mass a message was read from

Archbishop John Roach in the name of the U.S. bishops' conference: "On this second anniversary there are reasons to believe that their deaths have borne fruit." The text mentioned steps toward a negotiated peace. "In life, the work of the Jesuits helped make a negotiated solution possible; in dying, their sacrifice and example have given strength to all who seek peace.")

While they shine with good news, Fr. Tojeira continued, "they also shine as a denouncement of so much innocent blood which has flowed and continues to flow. They represent, along with many others, life which is trampled under foot. Joined with the life of Archbishop Romero and other contemporary prophets, they continue saying strongly [in the words of Romero]: 'Stop the repression. No soldier is obliged to obey an order contrary to the law of God. No one should obey an immoral law.'"

The provincial considered it "symbolic" that the FMLN's unilateral truce was going into effect "on this day when we recall the death of our brothers."

Later addressing the "lords of the weapons," Tojeira said that "the dead whom you kill enjoy good health, and they are the ones mainly who are defeating you more and more in all the forums. Not only are they defeating you, men of weapons, but they are defeating all those pharisees and hypocrites who continue to send money for the war from the United States and other countries."

The martyrs also teach us that "only the one who gives his life, saves it. To give oneself completely, to show that love is stronger than fear and death, not only gives testimony of courage but also opens paths of personal and social liberation. When all is said and done, any one of our murdered brothers could tell us that theology of liberation is nothing more than an effort, facing the cross of Jesus and the oppression of our brothers, to systematize the reasons we have to live.

"It is a personal liberation because in giving themselves to their daily work, to solidarity with others, and to the radical option for life and for all that is human, they overcame their defects and broke with tendencies to smallness and selfishness.

"It is also social liberation because that same self-giving and service to the poor, from their position in the university, took on a structural dimension, leading them to confront the authors of fear and to confront so many and so complex situations of injustice.

"Were our brothers theologians of liberation? They earned that title through their word, their writings, and their social commitment. But in shedding their blood they have gone beyond the title of theologian to become now a liberating grace for all of us and for every person of good will. Not only do they show us a reason to live, but now they themselves are reason for us to keep on living."

Fr. Tojeira then mentioned one of the most significant aspects of the celebration: that two young Jesuits had asked to be ordained in this anniversary Mass. "The bishop will tell them to 'imitate what you commemorate' as he hands them the chalice and paten. And now our young Jesuits will never forget, as they commemorate the death of the Lord until he comes, that the blood of Jesus gives meaning and is joined to the blood of Archbishop Romero, to the blood of the six Jesuits, to that of Elba and Celina, to that of our brothers and sisters of Mozote and Sumpul, and to that of so many anonymous Christians who have completed in their flesh 'what still remains of Christ's sufferings for the good of his body, the church' (Col 1:24).

"Peace is being built here in El Salvador. There is more and more reason to see this anniversary as a festive day and not a day of mourning. With all its limitations and delays, the dream which so many of our murdered brothers and sisters had is coming to pass: a definitive end to the war. What remains is the task of struggling peacefully but decidedly against the causes which gave rise to the war. Both are part of the same dream, the same hope.

"May all of us here present go forth," Tojeira concluded, "with a commitment to strengthen the peace process with our work, our word, and our solidarity—all with the same dream of a fraternal society where the good shine like bright stars and where there are reasons for living. May the Lord Jesus, the bright star from which our brothers received the light, the very solidarity of God with all and especially with all the crucified of this world, give us strength from his Eucharistic presence. And because of this strength may El Salvador be more and more worthy of the name it bears as a country."[3]

At the offertory, one of the items brought to the altar, as in the first anniversary Mass, was some of the blood-soaked earth from the yard where the Jesuits had been killed. "We offer you, Lord, our earth fertilized with so much sweat, suffering, and innocent death. It is watered with the blood of those who made their own the way of Jesus and that message pronounced by him: 'Whoever wishes to save his life will lose it, and the one who loses his life for my sake will find it.' That this gospel challenge may be fulfilled among us, let us pray to the Lord."[4]

---

[3] *Carta a las Iglesias*, November 16-30, 1991.
[4] *Ibid.*

The ordination rite for the two young Jesuits had a deep and obvious meaning for everyone. One traditional element of the ceremony had particular impact: when the ordinands lay down prostrate as a symbol of self-giving. The commentator noted aloud that the corpses of the slain priests were found precisely in that position. Did those about to be martyred remember the scene from their ordination and ponder how they were now carrying out their priestly and religious oblation to its ultimate consequences? Did they have time to remember how Jesus, in his agony in the garden, "threw himself face downward on the ground, and prayed, 'My father, if it is possible, take this cup of suffering from me! Yet not what I want, but what you want'" (Matthew 26:39)?

Unlike their Jesuit brothers martyred two years before, the two young Jesuits stood up again. They themselves were one of the offertory gifts: "We offer you, Lord, these new priests," a Jesuit proclaimed. "They wanted to be ordained on the anniversary of the day on which those eight brothers and sisters shed their blood and gave their lives. Juan Ramón Moreno reminds us: 'The good shepherd is the one who gives his life. In our world a price must be paid for taking up the cause of the poor, a price consisting of sharing the same lot and destiny of the poor: disdain, oppression, and repression. But what is important for the Church and for our religious institutes? To be well regarded and supported by the world, or to be a cry of hope, good news for the despised of the earth?' That we may not forget this distinguishing mark of the good shepherd, let us pray to the Lord."[5]

❄   ❄   ❄

---

[5] *Ibid.*

In his first Mass the next day, Fr. Guillermo Soto noted how the slaying of Fr. Rutilio Grande in 1977 planted the seeds of many vocations, including his own, and how it affected Archbishop Romero.

Fr. Carlos Manuel Alvarez chose to celebrate his first Mass in Ciudad Romero, a settlement of Salvadorans who returned home after ten years in exile in Panama. Carlos Manuel, who had done some pastoral work there during his final year in seminary, thanked the people for all they contributed to his development as a Jesuit. (As we drove into the settlement, I noticed a sign with the message: "No to the military presence." As we left, several government soldiers stopped and searched the bus.)

During my additional days in El Salvador I spent some moments in the university chapel, near the crypts in the wall where the six Jesuits are buried. An abundance of flowers and wreaths spoke of the people's love for them and their belief that the martyrs live. One wreath carried this message from the bookstore personnel: "These flowers which we offer today represent the life and work of our martyrs. Just as the flowers germinate and multiply, the thinking of the martyrs will keep flowering and expanding more and more in the hearts of those who form this university community."

From time to time throughout the day, people stopped in to spend some time near the martyrs. They wanted to be mindful of them, in their presence; they wanted a ray of light from those "bright stars" who offer a corrupt world the "message of life." They were contemplating the face of God in the martyrs, and finding goodness and hope.

"I frequently visit the blessed sacrament in the Romero chapel," a student wrote, "in order to accompany Jesus for a little while, to console him and to atone for what is being done to him. I believe that in the whole history of our country he has never been so offended as today. It is tremendous," she continued. "I feel sadness, pain, and most shame as I consider what we have been capable of doing, through the terrible sins.

"It makes us ask ourselves, how has it been possible? Distraught, I do not find words, but I let my heart speak. I seek the presence of Archbishop Romero and our martyrs. As I stay there in silence, I begin to open my heart to them; I let them share my anguish, my fear and lack of confidence. I almost go so far as to demand their help, because now our capacities fall short in the face of so much violence and injustice. We truly feel powerless, like a ship without rudder, whipped by the storm with its winds seeming like hurricanes."[6]

During those same days the staff of the Center for Theological Reflection (of which the fallen Jesuits had been the heart and soul) were able to celebrate the birthday of a staff member in a conference room of the center.

Reflecting later on the second anniversary, Fr. Jon Sobrino (who lived with the martyrs and would have been killed with them if he had not been teaching a seminar in Thailand) emphasized that "the martyrs of the UCA, Archbishop Romero, and many others are martyrs for the cause of the poor, that is, for defending the poor majority. In Christian terms this means that they are true martyrs for the faith in a God who has made the poor, the little ones, the tortured, the disappeared, and the massacred his own people.

"It is also very important to emphasize that the tombs and the rose garden have become places of pilgrimage, prayer, and conversion," he continued. (The rose garden is the yard where five of the Jesuits were

---

[6] *Carta a las Iglesias*, November 16-30.

massacred, where Elba's husband planted rose bushes in the blood-soaked earth.) People visit them "as if they are visiting holy places," Sobrino noted, "with silence, respect, and devotion. Many tears have been shed before the roses; but there has also been much gratitude expressed to the martyrs."

Sobrino told of a woman, "a veteran of the Christian base communities," who said: "I have been sad and without hope for many months now as I see how different our Church is from that of Archbishop Romero. This anniversary has restored hope to me." The miracles of the UCA martyrs and of all the other Salvadoran martyrs, in Sobrino's view, are like the miracles of Jesus: "hearts that are touched, changed, given new life.

"These martyrs by dying have given us life; they have become our light in this ecclesial generation of greater darkness; they have strengthened our spirit in an era in which there is more ordering than inspiring; they have become, finally, our joy in moments in which sadness and fear abound in the Church.

"Whatever may be the future of the Church and of the new evangelization," Sobrino concluded, "these martyrs are necessary for the continued creation of the Church of the poor, which is the Church of Jesus; and they are needed so that the new evangelization may be the old evangelization of Medellín and of the Gospel. Let us never forget that these martyrs are those who really maintain the credibility of the Gospel of Jesus."[7]

❄   ❄   ❄

---

[7] *Ibid.*

The roses planted by Don Obdulio, husband of Elba and father of Celina, now give off a pleasant scent where the odor of death had prevailed. (Obdulio died in June, 1994.) The garden has inspired poetry: "Obdulio has created a little garden, transforming the place where the bullet-riddled bodies were sown, the place which turned the world upside down in horror over the picture, the earth which they watered with their blood. The roses have multiplied; harvested, they come again in abundance. Thanks be to God and to this people—so many Obdulios, Elbas, Celinas, the true El Salvador; together they tend the roses of our liberation."

Dan Berrigan has written: "Sweet murdered mother, sweet child, thank you. In the life you have won, others will serve you, you will sit like a queen and her daughter at the banquet of God. Valiant Jesuits, my brothers, thank you. You stood where you were called, and fell where you must. May your prayer win, even for us, a measure of that virtue most rare in a world of gunmen and guns: steadfastness."[8]

On the Saturdays leading up to November 16, Mass was celebrated in memory of each of the eight martyrs—in the UCA, in Jayaque, in Ciudad Segundo Montes. A reporter noted: "The people do not forget the love of the martyrs, because in that love their own hope and dignity, their own commitment and faith are confirmed. This is seen in songs which are more joyful, in offerings made with more love, in petitions felt more deeply, and in homilies more alive than on other days. The hugs of peace are more deeply felt, and the Spirit of God is felt like a slight breeze: we were all better for having celebrated.

---

[8] *Whereon to Stand: The Acts of the Apostles and Ourselves* (Baltimore: Fortkamp, 1991), p. 272.

"Something, if even just a little, has rubbed off on us of the contagious goodness of Amando, the simplicity of Lolo [Joaquín López y López], the sweetness of Celina, the tenacity of Nacho [Ignacio Martín-Baró], the decidedness of Ellacu, the mildness of Pardito [Juan Ramón Moreno Pardo], the enthusiasm of Montes, and the motherly look of Elba. Archbishop Romero smiles as he looks down at us from his picture on the chapel wall, and Jesus of Nazareth becomes a little more present among us."[9]

❄   ❄   ❄

On September 28, 1991, a jury convicted Col. Benavides and Lt. Mendoza of murder, and they were later sentenced to 30-year prison terms; the other defendants were acquitted.[10] Benavides was convicted on all eight murder counts. Mendoza was convicted of the murder of 16-year-old Celina Ramos but acquitted on all the other murder charges. "The remaining defendants, including the confessed triggermen, were absolved of all charges."[11] (During oral arguments by the defense, some 200 demonstrators outside the Supreme Court building had chanted slogans in favor of the defendants, interrupting the process inside.) Higher officials were not touched; the U.S. government continued to withhold documents pertinent to the case, claiming their release would imperil national security.

---

[9] *Carta a las Iglesias*, November 1-15, 1991.

[10] Benavides and Mendoza were released from prison on April 1, 1993, due to an amnesty which was pushed through the Legislative Assembly just five days after the March 15, 1993, publication of the findings of the UN Truth Commission.

[11] Doggett, *op. cit.*, p. 199.

"Most of the independent observers who attended the trial later concluded that these verdicts defied both logic and the weight of the evidence," Doggett observed. "Lt. Mendoza, by all accounts, did not fire his weapon. There is no more reason to link Mendoza to the killing of Celina Ramos than to any other murder. Celina died embracing her mother, the Jesuits' cook, with whom she shared a sofa bed that night. It is highly likely that whoever killed Celina also killed her mother."[12]

Congressman Joseph Moakley said he could not "rule out the possibility that the military interfered with the outcome of the trial."[13] Doggett considered it noteworthy "that the conviction did not touch the powerful Atlacatl Battalion, the U.S.-created and trained elite unit that carried out the murders."[14]

Fr. Rafael de Sivatte, S.J., Scripture professor at the UCA, wrote: "The poor and the oppressed never manage to receive true justice. Archbishop Romero said it would be strange if, in a situation where the poor are being assassinated, their fate was not being shared by priests, religious men and women, catechists, and others of the Church. Something similar could be said of our martyrs: it would be strange if this case had produced the full truth when that never happens with the martyrs of the people. This is the consequence of having cast their lot completely with the poor and the oppressed.

"Let us pray that, in spite of all the efforts of this world to muddy our memories and to make us forget our martyrs, remembering them may

---

[12] *Ibid.*

[13] *Washington Post*, October 14, 1991.

[14] Doggett, *op. cit.*, p. 202.

continue to be subversive, producing the revolution of the gospel, the good news for the poor."[15]

❄   ❄   ❄

On November 9 Jon Sobrino, in the UCA chapel, read a letter he had just written to his dear brother in Christ, Ignacio Ellacuria: "We have just read from the gospel of Luke, where Jesus proclaims his mission to free the oppressed and to announce the good news to the poor (Luke 4:16-21). Thinking of this gospel, I have thought also of you. Jesus exercised a powerful attraction over you. You were fascinated with him. You were not given to sentimental expressions, of course, but one day you got emotional about that Jesus, and in public.

"In the midst of analyzing the life of Jesus, suddenly you lost your rational cool and your heart overflowed, as you said: 'Justice led Jesus to go to the very root of things, and at the same time he had eyes and a heart of mercy to understand human beings.' You then fell silent and concluded your talk about Jesus with these words: 'He was a great man.'

"What drew you to the Spiritual Exercises of St. Ignatius and to the theology of liberation and to Archbishop Romero was that in words or in deeds they spoke about Jesus and made him present. And you too, Ellacu, along with many other people in El Salvador, made Jesus present.

---

[15] *Carta a las Iglesias*, November 1-15, 1991.

"You reminded us of Jesus with your prophetic message, your defense of the poor, and your courage in taking risks. When in 1976 the powerful once again tricked the poor with an agrarian reform, you wrote that famous editorial 'At your service, my capital,' a strong and carefully reasoned denunciation of a new blow against the poor.[16] Even in the face of bombs on the campus clearly intended for you, you kept on to the end. Someone told me some months before your martyrdom: 'Since they killed Archbishop Romero, no one has spoken in this country like Fr. Ellacuría.'

"And you reminded us of Jesus with your utopia, with your way of seeing and speaking about the poor as a crucified people, the body of Christ in history. There are two expressions of yours that I have cited the most. The first is this: 'Our times are full of signs through which the God who saves history is making himself present.... The sign is always the people crucified in history, the continuation of the Servant of Yahweh.' The second is the way you took the three questions asked by St. Ignatius at the end of the meditation on sin and expressed them

---

[16] Martha Doggett (*op. cit.,* pp. 19-20) has pointed out that "densely populated El Salvador has long had one of the region's least equitable patterns of land tenure. Pressure for arable land by the nearly 60% of the population who remained landless in 1979 is often cited among the root causes of the current civil war. One study showed that six families held more land than 133,000 peasants together.

"On June 29, 1976, El Salvador's Legislative Assembly adopted a modest agrarian reform program which would have affected only four percent of the country's land.... The Jesuits publicly and forcefully backed the plan, drawing criticism from the Right as well as from the Left. By October the proposal was withdrawn by Pres. Molina in the face of vociferous opposition by large landowners. An historical ECA [*Estudios Centroamericanos*] editorial, '*A Sus Ordenes, Mi Capital,*' said that the 'most reactionary sector of capital, the agrarian sector, had won the battle.... After such an exaggerated show of strength and determination, the government ended up saying, At your orders, my capital.' " The UCA campus was bombed six times during 1976.

in a contemporary way in the face of the crucified people: 'What have I done to crucify the people, what I am doing to get them off the cross, and what should I do so that this people may rise from the dead?'

"Help us, Ellacu, to stick to what is basic, what is truly ultimate: to truly accept Jesus, his prophecy and his utopia. Keep reminding us of today's gospel, which moved you so deeply in your life: that the Spirit of God becomes present when we follow Jesus, when we open the eyes of the blind, free the oppressed, and announce the good news to the poor. Help us, and thank you."[17]

Ellacuria spoke of the Third World poor as the crucified. Archbishop Raymond Hunthausen of Seattle, who decided to withhold half his income tax as a protest against U.S. militarism, spoke of the First World crucifiers: "I say with deep sorrow that our nuclear war preparations are the global crucifixion of Christ."[18]

❄   ❄   ❄

Shortly after the anniversary celebrations, a young Jesuit wrote: "After the verdict in the case of our martyrs, we were filled with anger and confusion; we felt beaten down and asked ourselves what sense it

---

[17] *Carta a las Iglesias*, November 1-15, 1991.

[18] Michael Gallagher, *Laws of Heaven: Catholic Activists Today* (NY: Ticknor & Fields, 1992), p. 206. In the same speech at Notre Dame University, Hunthausen said: "In considering a Christian response to nuclear arms, I think we have to begin by recognizing that our country's overwhelming array of nuclear arms has a very precise purpose: it is meant to protect our wealth. The United States is not illogical in amassing the most destructive weapons in history. We need them. We are the richest people in history."

all made; seeing how difficult it is that there be true justice in our country, we were losing hope. But today we feel that hope and faith have returned to our hearts.

"All these days of remembering our martyrs have been moments of strength, of an injection of spirit. We have shared these days alongside our poor and humble people who have made the martyrs their own, who love and remember them, celebrating the second anniversary with joy, hope, faith, full of the simple and throbbing life of the disinherited of this world."[19]

❄ ❄ ❄

One of the signs of hope in El Salvador today is the existence of communities of those who have returned from political exile. In exile, they sharpened their social, political, and religious consciousness and deepened their communal ways of living and working. They bring these gifts to the construction of a new El Salvador.

During the anniversary events, a representative of the people's library of Ciudad Segundo Montes spoke: "We in the Segundo Montes community have a people's library which really was born of the people, of their effort and commitment. It belongs to everyone, not to just a few, and least of all to the librarian. When we went to Honduras, persecuted and worn out by the repression, we were struck by the fact that eighty-five percent of our people were completely illiterate and that the rest were only semi-literate. Our time there allowed us to organize and develop ourselves, which was not easy, since it is very

---

[19] *Carta a las Iglesias*, November 16-30, 1991.

hard to leave a life of individualism and to adapt to a communitarian life where everything is for everyone. There the idea of the library was born, and we began to develop it, and it is now in the Segundo Montes community, back on our own land, that we are bringing this community project along with greater strength."[20]

During the main Mass on November 16, another representative of this community presented flowers as an offertory gift. Segundo Montes had visited the community often in Honduras. "He told us that, as he looked at our community, its organization and work, he saw El Salvador's future. We want to say that our community remembers him very much and that we are working and struggling to make his words a reality and to win peace for all our Salvadoran people."[21]

On the same day at Ft. Benning, Georgia, "Indian chants, prayers, and protest speeches filled the air at the front gates as [seventy] protesters expressed their outrage against the U.S. School of the Americas," according to the *Columbus Ledger-Enquirer* (November 17, 1991). The peaceful protest was in remembrance of the UCA martyrs and also to remember the arrest and imprisonment of Fr. Roy Bourgeois and the Liteky brothers one year before.

---

[20] *Ibid.* The importance of land to the peasant is crucial throughout Latin America. As one Mexican peasant put it: "For me, salvation is the ability to leave a piece of land to my children" (Roy May, *The Poor of the Land*, Orbis Books.)
   [21] *Ibid.*

Aaron Two Elk, an Oglala Lakota Indian and leader of the southeast division of the American Indian Movement in Atlanta, joined two other Indians in a traditional Indian song. Elk, a Vietnam veteran, then told the crowd that "he realized, as he got older and wiser, that he was actually taught ways to oppress people by the same system that has oppressed his people for years."

Protesters chanted: "We know what this place is for, murder in El Salvador," and "Remember the Jesuits, and why they died."

Fr. Liam Collins of Macon, Georgia, "said the death of the slain priests cannot silence protesters' voices in speaking out on the unjust policy of training killers. 'If death cannot silence them, then neither can this line,' he said in reference to a white line which the military police ordered the crowd not to cross."

❄   ❄   ❄

Peace took a giant step toward becoming reality exactly two months later. On January 16, 1992, the FMLN and the Salvadoran government signed a peace accord which resulted in a cease-fire on February 1. The Armed Forces were to be brought under the control of the civilian government; the purpose of the military was defined as national defense. Within two years it was to be reduced by fifty percent. Its ranks were to be cleansed of notorious human-rights violators.

Domestic security forces were to be dissolved, to be replaced by a National Civilian Police open to participation by ex-soldiers of the FMLN. New mechanisms were to be established to insure respect for human rights and political freedom, with the UN playing an important role.

Some agreements were reached on socio-economic issues, but for the most part these remained to be worked out through the new democratic process. The FMLN was to become a civilian organization with recognition as a legitimate political party. Its hope, as well as that of other progressive social forces, is that significant socio-economic change can be brought about through political rather than military struggle.

According to Rubén Zamora, leader of the Popular Social Christian Movement and of the Democratic Convergence, and Vice-president of the Legislative Assembly, a change in U.S. policy toward El Salvador contributed to the peace process. The change had its roots in two important events in 1989: the November offensive of the FMLN, "which showed the U.S. that a military victory was impossible," and the assassination of the Jesuits, "which showed the U.S. that the Armed Forces the U.S. was supporting were incorrigible."[22]

❋   ❋   ❋

"The martyrs have not died in vain," wrote Mary Carry, coordinator of the Peace & National Priorities Center of Oakland County, Michigan, echoing a deeply felt conviction shared by other solidarity workers. "They live on, and their concern for the poor lives

---

[22] Interview in *Envío* (UCA: Managua), February. 1992.

on in the will of the people to continue to struggle for justice. It is a wonderful thing to see," she noted after a visit to El Salvador.[23]

Fr. Roy Bourgeois was released from prison in August 1992. Living in an apartment across the street from the main entrance to Ft. Benning, he continued to denounce the School of the Americas in his educational work and protest activity.[24]

In August 1992 the Central American Province of the Jesuits announced that it would request a legal pardon for the two military officers convicted of the UCA murders. Fr. Tojeira explained that the Jesuits wanted the full truth about the case to come out. The verdict convicting Col. Benavides and Lt. Mendoza left the following free: "those who said in their extrajudicial confessions that they had fired the deadly shots, those who bore the weapons, those who finished off three of the martyrs who were wounded in the first spray of gunfire [Elba, Celina, and Fr. López y López], and above all the intellectual authors— those who organized, planned, and ordered the assassination.

"These intellectual authors knew that the FMLN offensive was coming, and they designed a plan to eliminate those who wanted peace with negotiations and justice. From the start there were civilians ready to create the conditions for the assassination. The continuous and insistent call-ins to the national radio network [under Armed Forces control], demanding the death of the Jesuits and the deportation of Archbishop Rivera and Bishop Rosa, were not by chance. Nor was it by chance that those in charge of the network permitted this.

---

[23] Spring 1992 Newsletter of the Jesuit Volunteer Corps: Midwest (P.O. Box 32692; Detroit, MI 48232).

[24] For information about the School of the Americas, contact Fr. Bourgeois at S.O.A. Watch, P.O. Box 3330, Columbus, GA 31903. Tel: (706) 682-5369.

"At the same time, an 'elite' group of the Atlacatl Battalion is brought in to the Military Academy. Their first mission is to search the Jesuits' house, scouting out the terrain. Then, in spite of the raging offensive, these battle experts are kept in a situation practically of waiting, outside the zones of heaviest combat. Col. León Linares, Atlacatl commander at that time, testified before the judge that he insistently asked his superior officers to return these troops of his to the battle, but this did not happen until the morning of November 16. No one has explained to the judge why these soldiers were not returned to their natural place of combat.

"Their chiefs were saving them for the right moment, from Monday to Wednesday, just waiting. Right after the murders, without letting them rest, at 6 a.m., their superiors ordered them into the thickest of combat. All this shows clearly that there was a conspiracy of a group of colonels, with power in the army, who supported and organized the crime. It is not a question of one person's [Benavides'] individual decision.

"Afterwards they determined who would pay for the crime instead of them. Later they applied pressure in different ways so that the members of the Atlacatl battalion would be freed, with the only ones incriminated being the two officers of the Military Academy." Tojeira reiterated the Jesuits' demand that the criminal masterminds be brought to light and justice.[25]

❄   ❄   ❄

In October, 1992, the Jesuit-run Central American University in San Salvador issued a declaration entitled "Five Hundred Years of

---

[25] *Carta a las Iglesias*, August 1-15, 1992.

Injustice and Utopia." The statement began by recognizing that "what happened five centuries ago decisively changed history. Since then it has been possible to speak for the first time of one humanity from a geographical perspective and also, little by little, from a historical perspective. That new historical development could have made possible a greater and more fraternal unity of the whole human family, but that did not happen. Rather, history shows that the differences and the oppression within the human family have deepened. Moreover, what we now call the 'third world' or the 'south' began to take shape then."

After describing the destruction of the indigenous peoples and cultures and the theological coverup of that conquest, the document noted that what happened in 1492 was "not only a serious sin then, but it unleashed the greed of other nations to come to our continent and to others. The forms and protagonists change, of course, but not the basics. Spaniards and Portuguese were followed by the British, the French, the Dutch, the Belgians, and afterwards those from the United States, here and in other parts of the world, up to the present.

"In these five centuries there has been no change in the basic interest which the powerful countries have in the Third World: to enrich themselves and grow, even at the cost of and against the poor who are the legitimate owners of what the powerful want to get. Thus ambition becomes an idol which leads to depredation and pillage and, when necessary, to war and annihilation, as can be seen in the many invasions of the South by those of the North. Just to recall some recent events which are close to us, let us mention the presence of the United States in Grenada, Honduras, Nicaragua, Panama, and in our country."

While recognizing that some development and progress has also come from the North's involvement, the main purpose is usually its own self-interest. "To facilitate this imperialist movement, the Northern countries promote ignorance, disinterest, and even scorn of the Third World. Their most fundamental interest is not in human beings but in tourist sites, raw materials, cheap labor, toxic waste dumps far away....

"Today it is easier for human beings to know one another better, but this does not mean automatically that we are more united and much less that we live in greater justice and fraternity with one another. In 1992 humanity is well reflected in Jesus's parable of Lazarus and the rich man. The gap between rich and poor, far from diminishing, has doubled between 1960 and 1992. The North asks that we be patient and offers us the rich person's crumbs which, they say, will grow little by little."

The document quoted the martyred Fr. Ellacuría: "The powerful nations today say that they come to the Third World to make us 'rich' and 'democratic.' But these generous propositions hide a very different political and economic project. Democracy as defended by the United States is false and deceptive; as a universal value it has absolutely no importance for them." The hypocritical nature of this kind of "democracy" can be seen most clearly in places where violent conquest and domination are used to preserve the power structure.

It is not enough for the First World nations and churches to ask forgiveness, the university noted; there must be a firm purpose of amendment and reparation. "In other words, history must be reversed." But the model of progress which the North offers "is not desirable;" in fact, it "is immoral, since it is centered on selfishness and built over a multitude of victims and corpses. Moreover, that progress has not humanized either the rich countries or the poor ones. But even if it were desirable, it is not possible since the planet does not have sufficient resources for that kind of progress. The average U.S. citizen has the material value of fifty Haitians, and there are not the resources to allow the Haitians and the 3.5 billion poor of the world to attain the standard of living of U.S., European, and Japanese citizens.

"In 1992 we must decide to want to live together as a human family (utopia) or at least to survive (necessity). In these five centuries injustice and oppression have not been the whole story. There has also been resistance and creativity on the part of the Latin American peoples, and these have grown markedly in recent years as the recent history of our country has shown: immense creativity to survive, but also to work in common, to struggle for justice, to generate values of truth, hope, giving, mercy, love. Also, in the countries of the North the solidarity groups have grown, and there are new ways of thinking, new aid programs, and new policies of some governments."[26]

---

[26] *Carta a las Iglesias,* October 1-15, 1992.

CHAPTER 3

The Third Anniversary

"Reflecting on hope is perhaps our most direct means of
apprehending the meaning of the word 'transcendence,' for
hope is a spring, it is the leaping of a gulf. It implies a kind of
radical refusal to reckon possibilities. It is as though ... reality
overflows all possible reckonings; as though it claimed, in
virtue of some unknown secret affinity, to touch a principle
hidden in the heart of things, or rather in the heart of events,
which mocks such reckonings.... Hope is not only a
protestation inspired by love, but a sort of call, too, a desperate
appeal to an ally who is Himself also Love"
(Gabriel Marcel, *Being and Having)*.

On November 16, 1992, while celebrating the third anniversary of the
martyrs of the UCA, the people of El Salvador were also looking
forward to December 15, when the year-long peace process would see
the FMLN disarm the last of its contingents as the government also
complied, after some delays, with peace accords. "Both events are
closely connected," the editors of *Carta a las Iglesias* said, "since the

martyrs are at the same time the cruelest product of the repression and of the war and the most outstanding builders of the peace."[1]

While gratefully recognizing the conciliatory efforts of both sides in the war and the involvement of the United Nations, other governments, and Church and human rights organizations in the peace process, the editorial also emphasized that "the blood shed by the martyrs and the love with which they have covered this country are bringing us closer to peace. There is no doubt that the barbarity committed on November 16 became a cry which could not be silenced and thus accelerated the peace process."

This year the anniversary was a commemoration of *all* the martyrs of El Salvador, the "thousands of men and women who have generously given their lives for speaking the truth and unmasking the lies, for promoting justice and struggling against injustice, for denouncing the oppressors and defending the impoverished." The martyrs are the men and women of the poor majority who have been killed "because they have struggled in all justice against poverty and because the believers among them did that in the name of the gospel." Among the cloud of witnesses are named "Ita, Maura, Dorothy, and Jean, the most precious gift of the people of the United States." Elba and Celina are named, and then the Jesuit martyrs, "murdered for putting science, which usually enriches the rich, at the service of the poor."

The martyrs of specific places are named, such as the peasants of Aguilares where in 1977 "the soldiers profaned the body of Christ in the tabernacle of the church and the body of Christ in history by killing dozens of peasants."

---

[1] *Carta a las Iglesias*, November 1-15, 1992.

Remembering the martyrs must be above all "a denouncement of what was done, in order that the aberrations which we have lived in this country are never repeated, in order that no one of either side again points weapons to kill or terrorize Salvadorans, and above all in order that armies financed and trained by the United States, security units, and death squads never again plant terror and horror in our country." The editors expressed hope that the Truth Commission and the Ad-Hoc Commission would be able to ascertain the truth and expose it publicly "so that it never happen again."

But it is necessary to remember the martyrs above all "to keep them alive and so that they continue to be light and inspiration. They are the ones who, even today, give us the best introduction into the truth of our reality. Isaiah says that the Suffering Servant is the 'light of the nations,' and Paul proclaims that in Christ crucified there is 'wisdom.' The martyrs help us to know our reality in its depths and to have that 'primordial grasp of reality' of which Ellacuría spoke in a technical way. He himself put it more simply: 'in the crucified peoples, as in a mirror, we can know what we are by what we produce.' Please God that the United Nations and the governments of El Salvador, of the United States, and of the European and other countries keep this before their eyes: if they want to know how we are and how the world is, let them look upon the crucified ones.

"The martyrs are those who in a selfish society introduce mercy and love; in a society of victims and victimizers, introduce reconciliation; in an unjust society in which institutionalized violence is rampant, introduce justice and peace.

"Finally, these martyrs, so beloved and remembered in their communities on the one hand and so ignored and slandered among the powerful on the other, are at one and the same time God's gift to our people and the acceptable offering which rises to heaven from our country. The 'Divine Savior' is not only the patron and the name of our country, but many Salvadorans make him present in their lives and in their deaths. And Jesus (let it be said at least for the consolation of relatives and friends who have survived them) remembers them.

"The cross of our people and the blood of the martyrs is what continues to make the blood and the cross of Jesus present in history. Let the Church never forget them, and let it build itself as the Church of the poor and as the Church of martyrs."

❄   ❄   ❄

The anniversary celebrations customarily begin before November 16, with Masses dedicated to each of the UCA martyrs. The Mass in honor of Fr. Ellacuría was held on October 31, the date for the final demobilization of the FMLN forces. That event, however, was postponed to December 15 due to the government's inadequate compliance with the peace accords.

At the Mass on October 31 Fr. Jon Sobrino read a letter addressed to Fr. Ellacuría: "Today is October 31—here among us—and it is the day on which the peace accords were to have reached their conclusion. That is why we chose to remember you on this day.... But the accords have not been complied with. The forces of evil—the most extreme right wing—are now trying to destabilize the process.

"Let us recall how in 1976, when the first timid and humble steps of agrarian reform were taken, the president of the republic turned it back. Then you wrote one of your best editorials, which you entitled 'At your service, my capital.' Perhaps today you would have written one entitled 'At your service, my captain.' Because, with things going well, the armed forces have not wanted to yield."[2]

As on previous occasions, Mass was celebrated in the first hours of the 16th, coinciding with the hour of martyrdom. In the afternoon of the 16th, two thousand people took part in the Mass, with the archbishop and the papal nuncio presiding. Many politicians, ambassadors, priests, and religious participated, along with a sizeable group of ex-commanders of the FMLN.[3]

In the homily, the Jesuit provincial reiterated the Jesuits' intention that the celebration "be also and above all the feast of all the martyrs of El Salvador." All of them are the "true builders of this peace which is growing day by day, in spite of the efforts of some to impede it," said Fr. José María Tojeira.

"In the case of Jesus Christ, protomartyr who gives meaning to all martyrdom," he continued, "universal brotherhood, founded in the fatherhood of God, was clearly the supreme value—beyond laws, political interests, threats, brutality, and even beyond the religious constructs through which people try to systematize their response to God's call. For that brotherhood, Jesus peacefully took up the sin of the world. Trying to show us the way of fidelity to God in love of neighbor, he suffered the brutality of an unfraternal world which wanted and still wants to perpetuate itself through the law of the strongest, enslaving the little ones of this world who are the vast majority.

"But the death of Jesus immediately became the most radical denunciation of the sin of the world, and it became the creator of new brotherhood and the clearest and most lasting way of liberation in history.

---

[2] *Carta a las Iglesias*, November 16-30, 1992.
[3] *Ibid.*

Only fraternal solidarity, inspired in the fatherhood-love of a God who makes us all equal, is the authentic and permanent way of liberation.

"In El Salvador the martyrs, all the martyrs, are the ones who have followed the way of Jesus in the most radical way. They have written with their own blood that cry of Archbishop Romero which got him condemned to death: Stop the repression. And they have continued to shout out that message more strongly, because the killing of these peaceful ones brought out with perfect clarity the inhuman system of El Salvador in which the blood of one's brother is of less import than the jingle of money in one's pocket. Their sacrifice showed clearly that the system and the values which the executioners claimed to be defending was nothing more than a license to pillage, rob, kill, do business to benefit only a few, and to traffic in drugs, weapons, and lives.

"Why did they kill children in El Mozote[4], the elderly in Sumpul, women in Las Hojas, priests who never touched a weapon in the UCA and in so many other parishes, poor people and all kinds of people in so many places? Because they were afraid to lose their privileges, their businesses, and even, for some, their military rank. And today it is precisely all these martyrs massacred like Jesus who have the greatest power to question the idolatry of wealth, the greatest energy to demand the reform of a judicial system manipulated and sold to the strongest, and the greatest force to rid this country of evil.

"What do the martyrs ask of us who remain and who want to be faithful to their memory and their voice? A country, El Salvador, freed from the idolatry of wealth. Peasants with land, workers with work,

---

[4] A picture of exhumed skeletons of people killed at El Mozote in 1981 appeared on the front page, *The New York Times*, October 22, 1992. See Appendix Two on the massacre at El Mozote.

salaries with dignity, laws and politics at the service of the weakest. That no one be sacrificed for the luxury of a few. That people, with all their richness and dignity as children of God, be the center of the laws, the economy, politics, and social life.

"They also ask of us a country freed from war and from the mentality which gives rise to every kind of war, freed from brute force as a pattern of interpersonal relations. A country where the deep human needs for love, for understanding, and for help and encouragement by society have priority. A country where there is true dialogue, rooted in the needs of a people who want to unite freedom and solidarity; work, rest, and dignity; economic development and social development.

"They ask of us a country freed from hatred and from the longing for revenge, a country with truth, justice, and forgiveness. If only those brothers who, blinded by their idolatries, took the blood of others would recognize their faults and simply ask pardon. What more do we want but to know the truth in order to be able to forgive, in order to be sure of the repentance of the executioners, in order to have a guarantee that the end to the repression has now become a 'never again' signed by all on the basis of pardon and reconciliation?"

(Tojeira had previously announced that the Society of Jesus would request a pardon for the two military officers convicted of killing the UCA martyrs. But he had also challenged the Salvadoran Minister of Defense to a public debate to show him that there are indeed "intellectual authors" of that assassination who had to be brought to justice.)

"Some ask us to forget, but this is not in the spirit of the Gospel," he continued in his homily. "How will we forget our martyrs? How will we forget those who so loved their land and their farm that they stayed on it while others, with foreign advisers, planned scorched-earth operations?"

The provincial ended his homily with a joyful reference to the peace at hand. "Where sin abounded, grace and reconciliation must abound all the more, and our martyrs are witnesses of that. May the strength of Jesus, martyr and liberator, present in this Eucharist, who sums up and gives meaning to all these deaths in martyrdom, give us the strength and the courage to build this country in peace."[5]

❄   ❄   ❄

Reflecting on the experience of what was celebrated and on how it was celebrated, a young theology student wrote: "Without doubt we could call this a 'sacrament of the people.' It is a sacrament because in the celebration we experienced the presence of God in the history of his people, the closeness and friendliness of Jesus shown in his martyrs. And it was 'of the people' because we all had something to remember and celebrate and because what Archbishop Romero had said was shown to be true: 'If they kill me I will rise in the Salvadoran people.'[6]

❄   ❄   ❄

In 1992 I celebrated the anniversary of the martyrs at Xavier University in Cincinnati. The program for the memorial service bore the

---

[5] *Carta a las Iglesias*, November 1-15, 1992.
[6] *Carta a las Iglesias*, November 16-30, 1992.

title: "Challenge to North America from a People of Hope." Jesuit Father George Traub opened the service: "Today Xavier University is honored to recognize the value of the lives and the tragedy of the deaths of these eight individuals. While we might consider that the priest-professors knew and accepted the dangers inherent in their positions, the same cannot be said of Julia Elba Ramos and her daughter Celina. They had done nothing to attract attention, to bring punishment upon themselves, to think they were in danger. Their deaths symbolize the randomness, the unfairness, the senselessness of murder.... These now silenced servants symbolize those 70,000 innocent victims of the Salvadoran war—all those children, women, and elderly who without taking up arms have been cut down in the crossfire of El Salvador's disastrous decade-long war."

All then joined in prayer: "O God, who comes into our world to live among us, be with us as we gather before you to hear again the voices of your martyrs. In these voices, crying out with the suffering of your people in Central America, and all the poor of our world, help us to hear the challenge of your call, your demand, for justice in this broken world. The deaths of these martyrs come to us as a challenge from Central America to see our world through the eyes of the poor. Open our hearts to receive that challenge and to find in the struggle for justice hope for our world."

Various faculty members read excerpts from the words of the martyrs. Professor Irene Hodgson quoted Fr. Martín-Baró: "I really admire my people. I think it's difficult to survive, and still they are able to smile, to hope, to love, to pray, to say the Our Father even for their enemies. In the refugee camps, always in times of prayer the people who have lost relatives pray to God for their enemies, pray for them to become brothers. Maybe here my academic skepticism has to give place to religious faith, or to human faith in my people. And if I am able to enjoy life, it's because I learn from them friendship, solidarity, and to show faith."

Xavier University President, Fr. James Hoff, S.J., quoted Fr. Juan Ramón Moreno: "Yes, Christ is a subversive. He wants to subvert all those structures that have been built to defend selfish interests. He asks that they be changed and that the powers that accompany them be put at the service of all lives, be transformed from power into humble service. This is the essence of Christ's message. But the powerful resist that, seeing Christ as a threat and accusing him of being a subversive."

Professor Bill Daily gave a reading from the words of Fr. Ellacuría: "Today the university is tapped to awaken ever more hope, to show above all that there are solutions for the country, however difficult and costly they may be. Hope is not optimism alone, nor does it consist in hoping that others will resolve the problems. Sooner rather than later one has to put one's hands to work with disinterest, with lucidity, and also with sacrifice. The university must be one of the promoters of this work."

Later in the service Professor Daily quoted again from Fr. Ellacuría: "It is not that liberation theology or Salvadoran Jesuits are promoting violence. On the contrary, violence is what we are trying to overcome. But let us not deceive ourselves about where all this violence began. It started with what the Church called institutionalized, legalized violence, whether in the form of economic exploitation, political domination, or abuse of military might."

Professor Paul Knitter read the final quote, this one from Fr. Jon Sobrino, who would have been killed with his brothers if he had not been out of the country at the time:

"By the end of this century, one third of Latin Americans, some 170 million people, will live in poverty (or rather in normal, inhuman poverty), while another third will live in dire poverty.... The Third World offers the First World the possibility of conversion. If entire crucified continents do not have the strength to convert hearts of stone into hearts of flesh, we must ask ourselves, what can? And if nothing can, we must ask what kind of future awaits a First World built (consciously or unconsciously) upon the corpses of the human family.

"The solution is solidarity. We all need each other and we can all help each other. The history of relations between North and South is a sad history, but it can change, and in any case it must change. The North can and must help us to make that minimum of a just and decent life possible. The South can become a reserve of spirit for the North. What is important is to recover or begin to have the idea and the ideal of the human family."

After these readings, participants in the service shared their personal reflections about the martyrs. Then all recited: "The people of Central America have offered a challenge to us, inviting us to look at our world through their eyes. In that challenge is also our hope—because, once we know, once we see, we can become part of God's great act of redemption in our world, as God 'judges the poor with justice and decides aright for the land's afflicted, strikes the ruthless with the rod of justice,' as God creates a world, and we with God, in which there shall be no more harm or ruin on all God's holy mountain."

The service concluded with a prayer: "God, our redeemer, make us people of hope.... May the witness of your martyrs give us strength, calm all our fears, and fill us with the passion of your love."

Earlier in 1992 a group of Xavier University faculty and students had gone to El Salvador and Nicaragua to see first-hand the suffering of the poor and the effects of U.S. policy. In Nicaragua, the most powerful experience was a meeting and Mass with the mothers of the war dead— those killed in the struggle against Somoza and those killed in the war against the U.S.-sponsored contras. Each mother gave the name of her

Fr. Ellacuria's unpacked suitcases.

Newspaper in the reading room of the martyrs' residence. The headline reads: "Salvador Battles Claim 127 Lives."

Reading room of the martyrs' residence.

Room where body of Juan Ramon Moreno was placed by troops.

Room where Elba and Celina were killed.

Outside of room where Elba and Celina were killed; bootprints in blood.

Yard where Jesuits were killed; blood in grass and spattered on wall.

Front of Center for Theological Reflection, adjoining martyrs' residence.

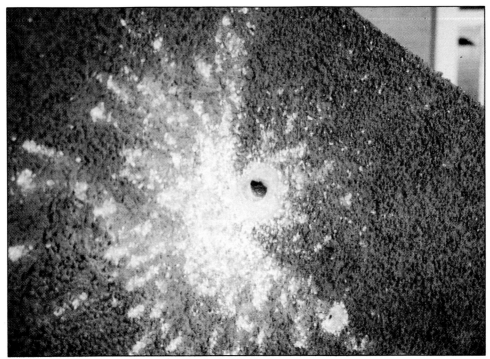

Outer wall of stairway on Center for Theological Reflection.

Inner side of same wall.

Destruction of office in Center for Theological Reflection.

Destruction of office in Center for Theological Reflection.

Damage to kitchen of martyrs' residence.

Bullet-riddled window of car in lot.

Picture of Fr. Rutillo Grande, S.J., in Center for Theological Reflection.

Charred picture of Archbishop Romero in Center for Theological Reflection.

Coffins of the martyrs in university chapel.

Coffins of the six Jesuits in university auditorium at funeral Mass. (Elba and Celina were buried in their home town.)

Jesuit provincial Fr. Jose Maria Tojeira in sermon at funeral Mass.

Archbishop Rivera y Damas at funeral Mass.

Crypts in wall of university chapel, under picture of Archbishop Romero.

Coffins placed in crypts in wall of university chapel.

Bodies of the martyrs on lawn of Center for Theological Reflection.

Bodies of the martyrs on lawn of Center for Theological Reflection.

son/daughter/spouse and where and when he/she was killed. One woman lost four sons and her husband! The Xavier group started crying about half-way through, and some of the mothers could not speak through the tears.

At the end of this, one member of the group said that in spite of all our efforts in the United States, we failed to stop the killing of their sons, and asked forgiveness (which they had already expressed in the non-violent way they had spoken their truth to us.) We said they had given us new inspiration and strength to continue to work for peace and justice. This was another instance where the poor "evangelize" us.

In December 1992 the final contingent of the FMLN forces was demobilized. The government, however, responded most inadequately to the Ad-hoc Commission's demand to remove certain military officers known as human-rights violators. Perhaps even more difficult than the clean-up of the armed forces is the "reconstruction of the country on the basis of justice. The New Testament says, and historical experience shows with perfect clarity, that the root of all evil is the lust for money. The conflict began in our country, in effect, with an oligarchy building a system of institutionalized injustice (the first great evil which greed produced); but this generated a repressive armed force at its service along with certain government agencies, a justice system, and certain communications media which broadcast the institutionalized lie in order to cover up the reality. Betting on peace, then, means working to overturn all these institutionalized aberrations."[7]

On December 15 El Salvador celebrated the end of the armed conflict. Daniel Ortega, former president of Nicaragua, and George Price, prime minister of Belize, after joining in the festivities, visited the crypts of the

---

[7] *Carta a las Iglesias*, December 1-15, 1992.

Jesuit martyrs in the UCA chapel. Ortega, who had also visited the tomb of Romero, said: "We have come on this occasion to reaffirm our commitment to the struggle of this people. We know that in the struggle of the Salvadoran people Archbishop Romero and the martyrs of the Jesuit community were a vital part of this process, because with their death they gave life and also hope to the struggle of the people." Ortega ended his talk by expressing his "recognition and love of the Jesuit brothers who gave their lives for the poor, for the people, for justice, freedom, and peace."[8]

❄   ❄   ❄

The report of the UN Truth Commission, issued on March 15, 1993, noted that the Commission had recorded 22,000 denunciations of serious acts of violence in El Salvador from January 1980 to July 1991. "More than sixty percent consisted of extrajudicial executions; more than twenty-five percent consisted of forced disappearances; and over twenty percent included denunciations of torture. The witnesses attributed almost eighty-five percent of all cases to government agents, to paramilitary groups allied with them, and to the death squads.

"Members of the Armed Forces were accused in almost sixty percent of the denunciations, members of security forces in approximately twenty-five percent, members of the military secret service (bodyguards) and of civil defense in about twenty percent, and

---

[8] *Carta a las Iglesias*, December 16-31, 1992.

death squad operatives in more than ten percent. In five percent of the cases the denunciations placed the blame on the FMLN."[9]

The Truth Commission was established by the government of El Salvador, the FMLN and the United Nations in the April 1991 Mexico round of peace talks. "The Commisson had a broad mandate to examine past abuses and document responsibility. Specifically, it was charged with 'investigating serious acts of violence which have occurred since 1980.'"[10] The Commissioners were former Colombian President Belisario Betancur, former Venezuelan Foreign Minister Reinaldo Figueredo, and U.S. law professor Thomas Buergenthal.

In reference to the killings of the Jesuits at the UCA, the report stated: "On the night of 15 November 1989, then-Colonel René Emilio Ponce [later to become a General and the Minister of Defense], in the presence of and in collusion with General Juan Rafael Bustillo, then-Colonel Juan Orlando Zepeda, Colonel Inocente Orlando Montano and Colonel Francisco Elena Fuentes, gave Colonel Guillermo Alfredo Benavides the order to kill Father Ignacio Ellacuría and to leave no witnesses."[11]   (On March 25, 1993, Ponce publicly denied the Commission's finding.)   The report continued: "For that purpose Colonel Benavides was given the use of a unit of the Atlacatl Battalion which two days before had been sent to search the priests' residence."

At an earlier meeting of officers at Joint Command headquarters on the evening of November 15, 1989, "Colonel Ponce authorized the elimination of ringleaders, trade unionists, and known leaders of FMLN,"

---

[9] From Madness to Hope: The 12-year War in El Salvador," Report of the Commission on the Truth for El Salvador, UN Doc. S/25500, April 1, 1993, at 43, hereinafter cited as "Truth Commission".

[10] *Ibid.*, p. 11.

[11] *Ibid.*, p. 46.

in the words of the Truth Commission. "The Minister of Defense, General Rafael Humberto Larios López, asked whether anyone objected. No hand was raised. It was agreed that President Cristiani would be consulted about the measures."[12]

Some officers stayed behind after the larger gathering. The Truth Commission said, "Colonels Ponce, Francisco Elena Fuentes (then commander of the First Infantry Brigade), Juan Orlando Zepeda and Inocente Orlando Montano, both vice-ministers of defense, and General Juan Rafael Bustillo, the Air Force commander, sat discussing decisions taken earlier. Ponce called over Colonel Benavides and 'ordered him to eliminate Father Ellacuría and leave no witnesses.'"[13]

Returning to the Military Academy, Benavides reported to his men on the decisions taken at Joint Command headquarters. After saying that he had been ordered to eliminate Ellacuría and leave no witnesses, Benavides asked any man who did not agree with the order to raise his hand; none did so. According to Doggett's summary of the Commission's findings, "Major Carlos Camilo Hernández, the acting Academy deputy director who was sentenced to a three-year jail term for his role in the coverup, organized the operation. His own Soviet-made AK-47 rifle was used, since having been captured from the guerrillas, it could not be traced. The use of the FMLN's most common weapon was one of several steps taken to implicate the guerrillas.

"Major Hernández assigned Lieutenant Edgar Santiago Martínez Marroquín, whose name had not previously surfaced in connection with the case, to coordinate troop movements in the area around the UCA. Confirmation of Martínez Marroquín's role suggests strongly that the

---

[12] Truth Commission, at 50.
[13] *Ibid.*

murder mission was a full-scale military operation using the armed forces' standard operating procedures. After curfew, in the midst of a guerrilla offensive, soldiers on duty would obviously have been under orders to shoot at anything that moved. Had they not been briefed that the Atlacatl would be passing through their lines, men stationed around the UCA would have engaged the Atlacatl commandos in combat. With these additional revelations, the Truth Commission report depicted a crime of much wider scope, involving more Army units and implicating the Armed Forces on an institutional level."[14]

Regarding the coverup, the Truth Commission found that "Col. Manuel Antonio Rivas Mejía, Head of the Commission for the Investigation of Criminal Acts (CIHD), learnt the facts and concealed the truth; he also recommended to Col. Benavides measures for the destruction of incriminating evidence."[15]

On the morning of November 16 Major Hernández and a lieutenant gave Chief of Staff Ponce a full report on the operation. They had with them a suitcase containing the $5,000 in prize money which Fr. Ellacuría had received in Spain. The officers told Ponce that the suitcase also contained photographs and documents. Ponce—recognizing that the existence of the suitcase implicated the Army in the murders—ordered its destruction, and those orders were carried out later at the Military Academy.

The Truth Commission attributed to the SIU an aggressive role in the coverup. After the murders, Col. Benavides confessed his role in the killings to SIU chief Lt. Col. Rivas Mejía, and secured his help. "Rivas told

---

[14] Doggett, *op.cit.*, p. 255.
[15] Truth Commission, at 46-47. (The CIHD is the official name of the Special Investigative Unit, or SIU.)

Benavides he should destroy the barrels of the weapons used in the crime, since the SIU would run ballistics tests on them. Atlacatl Commander Lt. Col. León Linares helped destroy the barrels. Rivas later tipped off Benavides that a request would be made for the Academy's logbooks, suggesting that Benavides eliminate anything incriminating in the registries. The logbook in which exits and entries to the Academy were recorded likely contained a notation indicating when the troops departed for the UCA on the murder night. Benavides ordered his subordinates to burn the books for 1988 and 1989."[16]

According to the Truth Commission, Col. López y López, who had been placed at the SIU by Col. Ponce, "learned what had happened and concealed the truth." (Buckland had also mentioned the role of López y López.)

The Truth Commission described how the SIU and the Military Honor Commission worked in concert under military control. "Lic. Rodolfo Antonio Parker Soto, a civilian attorney who works for the Armed Forces and served as counsel to the Honor Commission, censored the extra-judicial confessions made by the defendants. He was present when the SIU recorded the confessions and ensured that all references to higher orders and higher ranking officers were excluded, especially mention of Lt. Col. Camilo Hernández. Hernández and Ponce are said to have remained close since the younger man served under Ponce at the Third Brigade. Indeed, the AK-47 used to kill Fathers Ellacuría, Martín-Baró and Montes had been a personal gift from Ponce to Hernández.

---

[16] Doggett, *op. cit.*, p. 256. This account coincides with the testimony of U.S. Major Eric Buckland, who had been told by a Salvadoran officer that Benavides had confessed to Rivas and sought his help.

"By early January 1990, when the arrests were made, the High Command understood that some scapegoats needed to be offered up. The challenge was to craft a credible version of events which could serve as a basis for limited prosecutions, while insulating the High Command from the crime.

"Gen. Gilberto Rubio Rubio, who served as Chief of Staff until July 1, 1993, joined Generals Ponce, Zepeda and Montano throughout the two-year judicial process in pressuring junior officers 'not to mention higher orders in their testimonies before the court,' according to the report. Witnesses were regularly coached by ranking officers and their attorneys in preparation for sessions before the judge."[17]

❄   ❄   ❄

With regard to the murder of the four U.S. church women in 1980, the report (p. 66) noted substantial evidence indicating that the director of the National Guard and other officers "knew that members of the National Guard had committed the murders and by their actions facilitated the coverup of the deeds, obstructing the respective judicial investigation. Then-Minister of Defense, Gen. José Guillermo García, made no serious effort to investigate in depth the question of responsibility for the murders."

As for the El Mozote massacre in 1980, the report (p. 120) found that "it is completely proven that units of the Atlacatl Battalion killed, in a deliberate and systematic way, a group of more than 200 men, women, and children, which comprised the entire civilian population which they [the

---

[17] *Ibid.*, pp. 257-258.

troops] had found in the place the day before and which since then they had held in custody." (See Appendix Two.)

With regard to the murder of Archbishop Romero, the Truth Commission (p. 127) concluded: "Ex-Major Roberto D'Aubuisson [founder of the ruling Arena party] gave the order to assassinate the archbishop and gave precise instructions to members of his security corps, acting as a death squad, to organize and supervise the assassination." Other military officers are named as "having played an active role in the planning and carrying out of the murder."

Analyzing the origin of the death squads, the report noted that "ex-Major D'Aubuisson gained great support from civilian personages with vast economic resources who feared that their interests were affected by the reform program announced by the government junta.   They were convinced that the country was seriously threatened by a Marxist insurrection which they had to defeat.   The Truth Commission obtained much testimony that some of the large landowners and wealthiest business persons inside and outside the country made available their farms, homes, vehicles, and bodyguards to help the death squads.   They also gave money to organize and maintain the squads, especially those directed by ex-Major D'Aubuisson....

"Because of their clandestine way of proceeding, it is not easy to establish all the links between the private business sector and the death squads.   But the Truth Commission has not the slightest doubt about the close relation and the danger for the future of Salvadoran society that business people or members of the wealthy families may feel the need and could act, as in the past, with impunity in the financing of paramilitary killer groups."

The report also noted that "the government of the United States tolerated, apparently with little official attention, the conduct of Salvadoran exiles living in Miami, especially between 1979 and 1983. This exile group financed directly and helped indirectly to lead some of the death squads, according to testimonies received by the Commission. It would be useful if other investigators, with more resources and more time, would clarify this tragic history to assure that there is never again in the United States such tolerance of persons linked with acts of terror in other countries."

The government of El Salvador, "through the actions of members of the Armed Forces and/or of civilian officials, is responsible for having participated in, promoted, and tolerated the functioning of the death squads which attacked in an illegal way members of the civilian population."

The Commission insisted: "It is necessary to clarify the relation beween members of the private business sector, along with some wealthy families, and the financing and use of the death squads.... The matter of the death squads in El Salvador is of such importance that it requires a special investigation. It is especially important that more resolute action be taken by national institutions with the collaboration and assistance of foreign agencies which may have information about this matter. In order to verify a series of concrete violations and to place responsibility it will be necessary to investigate the serious acts of violence committed by the death squads case by case."[18]

❄   ❄   ❄

The day before the report's release, President Cristiani appeared on TV calling for "maturity and patriotism," while indicating his intention to

---

[18] Truth Commission, pp. 134-138.

implement an immediate general amnesty. On March 20, ARENA assembly deputies, with the support of two other conservative parties, passed an unconditional and far-reaching amnesty. Doggett considered it odd that the amnesty included a chapter in the penal code dealing with crimes committed by lawyers and judges, "none of which fall within the definition of political crimes eligible for amnesty. Perhaps fearful that the Truth Commission's emphasis on judicial complicity in impunity might result in prosecutions of civilian officials, the law's authors expanded the scope of 'political offenses' to include crimes such as coverup and willfully improper judicial rulings."[19]

Archbishop Rivera y Damas rejected the amnesty and expressed concern about the "desperate maneuver of the government to forget and maintain impunity in [the Archbishop Romero case] and other cases."[20] Jesuit provincial Fr. Tojeira termed the amnesty an "affront to justice."[21]

On March 31 a court ruled that the amnesty applied to those convicted in the Jesuit case, and the next day Col. Benavides and Lt. Mendoza walked out of prison. This fulfilled the recommendation of the Truth Commission that the two men should not remain in jail while others responsible for planning the killings and carrying them out remained free. The cases against the others convicted on lesser charges were dropped.

---

[19] Doggett, *op. cit.*, pp. 271-272. The government showed its defiance of the Truth Commission again on May 20 when police opened fire on a march by disabled veterans (of both sides), killing three and wounding twelve others. Two of the three dead were disabled veterans of the government's Armed Forces. (*Carta a las Iglesias, 16-31 de mayo*, 1993.)

[20] Radio YSAX, March 21, 1993.

[21] *El Pais*, April 12, 1993.

Col. Lopez y Lopez and Col. León Linares (who headed the Atlacatl Battalion in November 1989) were placed on "unassigned" status in April 1993. It was widely believed that these moves were linked to the "purge" called for by the Ad-Hoc Commission. Gen. Montano had earlier become Military Attaché in Mexico; Col. Francisco Elena Fuentes went to Guatemala as envoy to the Central American Defense Council.

On July 1, Generals Ponce, Zepeda, Rubio, and Vargas retired with full military honors, after 30 years of service in the Armed Forces, with President Cristiani expressing gratitude and praise for them. Gen. Bustillo, who had unexpectedly resigned as commander of the Air Force six weeks after the Jesuit murders, had resigned from the military in 1991.

Secretary General, Boutros-Ghali informed the Security Council on July 7, 1993, that the Salvadoran government was now in "broad compliance with the Ad Hoc Commission's recommendations, although with a delay of several months." According to his letter, the fifteen officers had been "placed on leave with pay pending completion of the procedures for their retirement, which would take place not later than 31 December 1993."[22]

Commenting on the retirement of the High Command and the departure of the *tandona* (the large graduating class of 1966), Fr. Rodolfo Cardenal, S.J., said: "We cannot say that they have been forgiven without their having recognized their role in the events. This would be to forget and we cannot do that.... They have not demonstrated that they want to be forgiven.... They have prevailed over civil society, retiring when they wanted to and in the manner they chose. And it's no secret they are leaving with their pockets full."[23]

---

[22] Doggett, *op. cit.,* pp. 276-277.
[23] *Diario Latino*, July 3, 1993, as cited by Doggett, p. 278.

CHAPTER 4

The Fourth Anniversary

The fourth anniversary of the UCA assassinations focused as much on the troublesome present as on the horrible past. Since the signing of the peace accords in January 1992, 24 FMLN members had been assassinated. Two prominent FMLN leaders were murdered in October, seriously jeopardizing the peace process as it moved toward the March 1994 elections. From January through October, 53 corpses showing evidence of torture were found; during the same period, 304 others were murdered by "unknown individuals" in circumstances similar to those which have characterized death-squad activity.[1]

Amnesty International expressed concern about the "alarming number of apparently political assassinations and death threats aimed particularly at FMLN members."[2] The Cristiani administration showed little interest in investigating and stopping this political terrorism of the right.

---

[1] Report by the Central American University's Institute of Human Rights, *Proceso*, November 17, 1993.
[2] *Ibid.*

The U.N. Truth Commission report, issued in March 1993, had demanded prosecution of those involved in death squads, but the government had proclaimed a defiant amnesty just before release of the explosive report. At the time of the fourth anniversary, two Jesuits and twenty others had been fasting for over two weeks in a church in Chalatenango, demanding the exposure and dismantlement of the death squads.

"We must go back to the Truth Commission report," stated the UCA's bulletin *Proceso* (November 3, 1993). "The past will continue to be present until it is confronted and exposed before national and international public opinion."

The fact that "the death squads have returned with impunity is partly a consequence of the government's failure to comply with the peace accords and with the recommendations of the Truth Commission. Some of the responsibility for this is also shared by the U.N. peace commission with its 'excessive diplomacy' and by the FMLN with its not very forceful posture" (*Proceso*, November 10, 1993).[3]

Why this resurgence of the death squads? According to polls, the main electoral contender against the ruling ARENA party was the Democratic Convergence/FMLN coalition. The death squads seemed to be an attempt to provoke the FMLN into a violent response which would

---

[3] Presidential candidate Rubén Zamora would later state: "Once the negotiations achieved one of their central objectives—an end to the armed struggle and the closing of any possibility of continuing the armed conflict—the ARENA government lost all interest in complying with the rest of the accords, which are those which will make this transition possible" (*Envío*, *UCA Managua*, marzo 1994).

tarnish its civil image and an attempt obviously to intimidate its members and supporters.[4]

In its statement on the occasion of the fourth anniversary, the UCA board of directors explained the resurgence of the death squads as the fruit of an alliance between recalcitrant sectors of the military and the old oligarchy. Some officers "do not accept the new role of the armed forces in a democratic society and fear that if the democratic forces gain more space in the government and in the legislative assembly they could even extend the scope of the military reforms." The discontent of certain right-wing sectors "could stem from the economic displacement to which they have been subjected by the financial and industrial right [the modernizing capitalist sector, represented by the circle of President Cristiani]. The former have been excluded by the latter from the benefits of the neoliberal economic policy and would not be prepared to face the inevitable transformations of Central American integration."[5]

The fast in Chalatenango ended on November 23 when an agreement was reached to form an independent commission consisting of government and UN representatives to investigate the death squads.[6] In early December, however, seemingly in defiance of this commission, another FMLN leader was assassinated.

Other troublesome signs included the stagnation of the Socio-economic Forum (due to the private sector's intransigence), the lack of

---

[4] *Envío* (*UCA-Nicaragua*), Noviembre 1993.

[5] *Carta a las Iglesias*, 1-15 de noviembre, 1993.

[6] One serious limitation on the work of this commission is that it had only six months in which to complete its investigation; another is that its scope was restricted to death-squad activities which occurred since the signing of the peace accords of January 1992. This latter restriction prevented this commission from fulfilling the mandate of the Truth Commission.

progress in land transfers, and the failure to quickly and effectively deploy the new National Civil Police.[7] In October evidence was revealed of collusion by the phone company and the armed forces in tapping conversations.

Furthermore, the government showed only token compliance with the agreement to purge the armed forces. Eight military officers mentioned by the Truth Commission as systematic violators of human rights were still on active duty. "The military does not recognize nor does it ask pardon for the horrendous crimes it has committed. Furthermore, it twists the situation and presents itself as the offended party. Officers can retire as honorable patriots, with impunity and with great economic benefits. The Supreme Court has shown equal stubbornness in refusing to accept its responsibility for the corruption of justice.

"General Bustillo, head of the air force when it was bombing the poor barrios during the November 1989 FMLN offensive and also an accomplice in the decision to kill the Jesuits at the UCA, went on to become a presidential candidate. (He subsequently dropped out of the race.) Former minister of defense General Ponce, named by the Truth Commission as responsible for the Jesuit murders, who publicly lied about it during all this time, was able to retire gracefully. The president of the Supreme Court said that God alone could remove him from his high post. And on the level of day to day living the people have suffered another blow to their hope: a steep hike in the price of beans." There was also criticism of the FMLN for its infighting, political compromises, and arms caches found in Nicaragua and El Salvador.[8]

---

[7] Letter to the Churches (English Edition), May 1-15, 1993.
[8] *Carta a las Iglesias*, 16-31 de julio, 1993.

❄   ❄   ❄

In November thousands of U.S. government documents regarding El Salvador were declassified in response to a congressional request that information concerning the thirty-two cases examined in the UN Truth Commission report be made public. The documents provide "powerful evidence that the Reagan and Bush Administrations collected detailed information about assassinations conducted by right-wing leaders in El Salvador in the 1980s but continued to work with them nonetheless."[9] In these documents, Cristiani's Vice-president, Francisco Merino, is mentioned as one of the organizers of the death squads. The documents also indicate that in 1981 a kidnapping was organized in the home of Armando Calderón Sol, who later became mayor of San Salvador and was elected president of the country in April 1994.

The CIA described Roberto D'Aubuisson to the Reagan Administration in its opening days as "principal henchman for wealthy landowners and a coordinator of the right-wing death squads that have murdered several thousand suspected leftists and leftist sympathizers during the past year." The CIA reported that D'Aubuisson trafficked in drugs, smuggled arms and directed the meeting that planned the assassination of Archbishop Romero. "The documents indicate that the Reagan and Bush Administrations sought nevertheless to keep on good terms with Mr. D'Aubuisson," according to *The New York Times*.

In 1984 the Reagan administration in a report to a Republican congressman downplayed the link between D'Aubuisson and the Romero killing even though, as the declassified documents show, a CIA

---

[9] Clifford Krauss, *The New York Times* (International), November 9, 1993.

report to Vice President Bush had characterized the allegations of a link as "credible." The documents "show that the Bush and Reagan administrations received intelligence reports that the Salvadoran military, which received $1 billion in United States military aid to fight leftist guerrillas between 1980 and 1991, was dominated throughout the decade by officers who either ordered or took part in death squad activities at some time in their careers."[10]

The papers also show "that the United States knew that the recently retired Defense Minister, Gen. René Emilio Ponce, worked with D'Aubuisson-led death squads when he was traffic police chief and an intelligence officer in the early 1980s." (The UN Truth Commission found that Ponce ordered the assassination of the Jesuits in 1989.) The papers "indicate that Defense Secretary Dick Cheney strongly opposed suggestions by Ambassador Walker and other State Department officials in 1991 to withhold military aid to protest delays in the investigation of the murders of six Jesuit priests. Over Bush Administration objections, Congress withheld more than $40 million in military aid to El Salvador in 1991."[11]

Doggett observed that "throughout the Jesuit case, U.S. officials had publicly sent a series of mixed messages, with some branches of the government working against the efforts of others." The documents, however, provide "a more coherent panorama, with U.S. officials attempting to protect their closest Salvadoran allies—namely President Cristiani and the military High Command—reacting belatedly to events as they unfolded and engaging in at times frantic damage control."[12]

---

[10] *Ibid.*

[11] *Ibid.*

[12] Martha Doggett, "The Assassination of the Jesuits: What the United States Knew," Latin American Studies Association, Atlanta, GA, March 10, 1994.

According to Doggett, U.S. Ambassador Walker met with the Jesuit provincial, Fr. Tojeira, five days after the crime. Tojeira "told the ambassador that he believed the Salvadoran Armed Forces had killed the priests, to which Walker replied, 'Yes, I think it's a special unit over which we have no control.' Yet the ambassador and other U.S. officials continued to suggest publicly that the killers could just as easily have been the FMLN."[13]

Before U.S. Major Eric Buckland came forward with his testimony about the reported involvement of Salvadoran Col. Guillermo Benavides in ordering the crime, the Embassy's legal officer Richard Chidester, "who functioned as the point person within the Embassy on the Jesuit case, argued that guerrilla combatants could have slipped through Army lines by traveling along a ravine, occupied the UCA campus for several hours and then killed the Jesuits. He maintained this theory despite the fact that the killers used an inordinate amount of firepower, shot bullets from an M-60 stationary machine gun, set fire to the building, shot off flares, etc., all in an area under military control....

"Once Col. Benavides was implicated in the crime, Mr. Chidester substituted Benavides for the guerrillas, using the same ravine theory to explain how Benavides' men could have reached the UCA without being detected by the some 300 other troops stationed around the campus. Under this revised scenario, Chidester acknowledged that Benavides was involved, but argued strenuously that he was acting on his own and not following higher orders."[14]

With regard to the documents released by the State Department in November 1993, Doggett noted that they "report for the first time that

---

[13] *Ibid.*
[14] *Ibid.*

a Salvadoran officer told the Embassy shortly before the case came to trial that Janice Elmore,[15] a political/military officer in the Embassy's political section, may have had prior knowledge of the plot to kill the Jesuits." Doggett cited a cable to Washington dated September 20, 1991, which "says the officer claimed Elmore 'either had prior knowledge of the murders or at least was aware of the existence of the so-called Jakarta plan,' a plot to kill prominent Salvadoran opposition figures. The source told the Embassy that Atlacatl Lt. Espinoza, who led the murder operation, had included the information about Elmore in a letter sent to the United States which was to be publicized if he were convicted; he was acquitted a few days later at trial."[16]

One indication that some U.S. personnel "might have gleaned useful information from Salvadoran colleagues was the testimony of Maj. Samuel Ramírez, a U.S. operations advisor attached to the training center for immediate reaction battalions adjacent to Atlacatl headquarters. A secret cable sent from San Salvador on November 21, 1990, informs Washington that a 'source of undetermined reliability' had alleged that Ramírez knew in late November or early December 1989 that the Atlacatl Battalion had murdered the Jesuits. Ramírez had informed his superior, Lt. Col. Fred M. Berger. Neither man had informed the Embassy's political staff, according to the allegation." The cable, signed by Ambassador Walker, concluded that the allegations should be investigated.

---

[15] Elmore accompanied Col. Menjívar, the U.S. MilGroup commander in El Salvador, on his January 2, 1990, visit to Joint Command headquarters where he laid out Maj. Buckland's story to Col. Ponce, as Doggett noted in *Death Foretold, op. cit.,* p.224.

[16] Doggett, "The Assassination of the Jesuits...", *op. cit.*

Interviewed by the FBI on December 20, 1990, "Ramírez stated that he worked closely with Lt. Espinoza, who served as a point of contact with U.S. trainers. Ramírez also revealed that without authorization the Atlacatl commandos had taken with them to San Salvador night vision equipment belonging to the U.S. trainers."[17]

In August 1990 Ambassador Walker "informed Assistant Secretary Bernard Aronson that the Moakley Task Force had received information implicating the High Command in the murders and orchestrating an extensive coverup," Doggett noted. "Walker urged the State Department to approach task force staff to 'get a sense of what the Moakley Commission will do with the information—and when. I have several concerns which I know you share: 1) that we do not act precipitously and irretrievably burn our relationship with Ponce at this critical stage; 2) that we do not imperil El Salvador Armed Forces cooperation on the peace process through unreasonable pressing for action on the Jesuit case; 3) but at the same time that we do not let the (Salvadoran military) get the impression that it can continue to stonewall on its involvement in the case.'" U.S. officials believed that Ponce "was key to gaining military acceptance to a peace accord."[18]

Looking at cables from the Defense Intelligence Agency and other military sources in San Salvador, Doggett noted that these documents "indicate that most Salvadoran military interlocutors told the North Americans that Col. Benavides did not act alone. Secondly, it is clear that an overwhelming body of evidence was gathered by both the

---

[17] *Ibid.* In *Death Foretold* (p. 331) Doggett pointed out that on December 12, 1990, Ramirez told a Salvadoran court: Lt. Espinoza "is the person I went through to coordinate the training, the requirements, the bedding, the food we were going to need for the special forces team that was going to come down."

[18] *Ibid.*

embassy and military and intelligence sources indicating that Lt. Col. Camilo Hernández, whom the judge charged simply with destruction of evidence, was heavily involved in the murder plot itself. A 'Secret' cable dated December 3, 1990, quotes the 'High Command's designated emissary' to the embassy on the case saying that the 'consensus at the highest levels of the Salvadoran Armed Forces' is that Hernández 'shares equal guilt as an intellectual author of the crime.'"

A March 1991 embassy cable to Washington referred to Hernández: "We and others have long suspected that he was very important in planning the murders but feared that he enjoyed the protection of Gen. Ponce and was immune from prosecution."[19]

Publicly, however, U.S. officials said they had no information linking others to the crime beyond the nine defendants. Asked after the jury trial if Benavides' conviction indicated a coverup of the role of higher ranking officers, State Department spokeswoman Margaret Tutweiler said that "if more evidence exists" the Salvadoran authorities should investigate. She added "that the United States had no knowledge of such evidence." The Truth Commission found that Lt. Col. Hernández "organized the [murder] operation."[20]

In a reference to the Salvadoran government's tendency to want to let bygones be bygones, an UCA editorial shortly before the fourth anniversary noted that "postmoderns and neoliberals are asking us to move beyond remembering and reflecting on the martyrs. But in this they are forgetting two things. First, in our country there are still an average of three murders a day, and many of these are killed by the same assassins as before (death squads, security forces, etc.), with the

---

[19] *Ibid.*
[20] *Ibid.*

same impunity as before, with the same methods as before, and above all for the same reasons and purposes as before.

"Secondly, many of the Salvadoran martyrs died **in continuity** with their life, so that, to forget their death is the most effective way to forget their life. It is true that martyrs die very heroically, but previously many of them lived very humanly; thus their heroic death was the **culmination**—not an absurd ending tacked on—to their complete Salvadoran and Christian life. And we are still absolutely in need of that kind of life in this country."[21]

The life and martyrdom of his wife and daughter gave Don Obdulio "great strength to continue struggling, to continue giving testimony," as he himself put it. Asking himself why God allowed him to live, the response he always found was that "he allowed me to live in order to give testimony of what happened that day." He further explained: "The blood shed by the Jesuit fathers was a step toward achieving peace. The blood shed by Elba was a step toward gaining respect for women in El Salvador, and the blood shed by Celinita encourages young people to demand respect."[22]

As in previous anniversaries, a Mass was celebrated in memory of each of the martyrs one day a week for eight weeks. In a Mass on the afternoon of November 15, the university community expressed its ongoing commitment to the ideals of the martyrs and offered its research and teaching to the Lord and the people. University president, Francisco Estrada, S.J., expressed gratitude especially for strides made by the UCA in training grass-roots public health promoters.

---

[21] "The Martyrs Teach us to Live," *Carta a las Iglesias*, 16-31 de octubre, 1993.
[22] *Ibid.*

A vigil was held throughout the night, with several thousand participating. Songs, traditional dances, and dramatic presentations nourished a spirit of hope and commitment. Mass was celebrated in the very first hours of the 16th. As in previous years, the words of consecration were heard as an expression of self-giving by Jesus and by his companions who had so often pronounced those words. While the vigil was being held on campus, thousands of people marched in the streets demanding the full implementation of the peace accords, action on the recommendations of the Truth Commission, and an end to the death squads.

The principal Mass began at 5 p.m. on November 16, with Archbishop Arturo Rivera y Damas, the papal nuncio, Fr. Tojeira, and about 20 other priests concelebrating and with a large throng participating. In the liturgy of the day (that of the Jesuit martyrs of Paraguay), the first reading was from Philippians 2:12-18: "So then, my dearly beloved, obedient as always to my urging, work with anxious concern to achieve your salvation, not only when I happen to be with you but all the more now that I am absent." No one could avoid hearing those words as if they were coming in a letter from Ellacuría or the other martyrs.

St. Paul urges the people to prove themselves "innocent and straightforward, children of God beyond reproach in the midst of a twisted and depraved generation—among whom you shine like the stars in the sky while holding fast to the word of life." The depravity of certain sectors of Salvadoran society (and their international allies) did not need to be underlined. The martyrs shine because of their affirmation and defense of life, and the faithfulness of the survivors gives the martyrs cause to boast that they "did not run the race in vain or work to no purpose." Their voices blend with St. Paul's in saying:

"Even if my life is to be poured out as a libation over the sacrificial service of your faith, I am glad of it and rejoice with all of you. May you be glad on the same score and rejoice with me!"

Psalm 27 proclaims the conquest of fear: "The Lord is my life's refuge; of whom should I be afraid?" The Salvadoran army itself attacked the UCA and murdered the martyrs: "Though an army encamp against me, my heart will not fear; though war be waged upon me, even then will I trust." The psalmist asks "to dwell in the house of the Lord all the days of my life," gazing on the loveliness of the Lord and contemplating his Temple. The martyrs gazed on the loveliness of the Lord in the bloody faces of the tortured and in the malnourished bodies of the poor; they contemplated the scarred world and suffering humanity as the Lord's temple and struggled to cleanse it of corruption, violence, and injustice. Only after walking that Calvary do they now gaze on the loveliness of the Lord himself, "hidden in his abode in the day of trouble" (v. 5).

Jesuit provincial Tojeira gave a relatively short but challenging and courageous homily. Why the insistence on remembering the martyrs? "What the world hates, it tries to destroy, to bury in silence, or to sweeten its memory. On the other hand, the followers of Jesus must, as he did, give testimony to the truth in this world. The first great martyr of truth was Jesus of Nazareth, condemned to death for colliding with the political, economic, and religious interests of his time who opposed the demanding relationship with a God who as Father would make all of us brothers and sisters. Out of that relationship with the Father and with his brothers and sisters, Jesus was the light of the world, but his light revealed too much hypocrisy, falsehood, lukewarmness, and injustice. The institutionalized lie could not stand his message."

After referring to the special place of the martyrs in the Church throughout history, Tojeira suggested that certain "aspects of our reality are reflected in the gospel we read today [John 15:18-21;16:1-3], which speaks of a world hostile to Christian truth. What are the death squads if not the world closed in on itself, selfishness hardened in stone in personal or group interests, which does not hesitate to destroy at whim what is most sacred, human life?

"In effect we live in a society in which very powerful sectors hate the truth. Certain kinds of killers are first hidden by the authorities, then officially protected, and finally, when the national and international outcry makes it impossible to keep them in their positions, they are retired with promotions and honors. We live in a society of mistrust in which even the president of the republic has his phone tapped. We live in a society which systematically confuses good with evil according to convenience: which seeks the support of the CIA to teach some how to eliminate their opponents and which becomes outraged and rends its garments when criminal complicity is made public. This is a society in which those who have certain amounts of power can lie, rob, or kill with impunity, and in which sufficient proof is never found against the big perpetrators of these crimes."

Tojeira also mentioned issues like "social injustice, the lack of jobs, lack of security, the hypocritical control of some of the communications media by those with evil intentions, the poverty which damages human dignity, and the squandering by the few which in this context becomes an insult.

"In the face of this reality which is so disheartening for many, it is important to remember the martyrs who are witnesses to humanity and to Christian identity.... They show us a path of consistency in the face of a reality which must be transformed, changed, radically changed.... We are indebted to them for the good portion of the peace which we enjoy today.... The bad portion, which we have described, is due to the executioners who remain imbedded, without conversion, in the social, political, or economic structures of our country. It is due to those who want to bury the martyrs in oblivion....

"Their generosity alone shows us the path of the future: a future where truth is virtue, justice is the norm, solidarity a spontaneous attitude, and austerity the foundation of a more human economy. A future in which we can pray the Our Father in a way which is consistent with the coming of the Kingdom for which we pray, in a way which is in keeping with the brotherhood and sisterhood derived from our daily bread shared by all, in a way which is consistent with a forgiveness which becomes the way of liberation from every evil.

"May the Lord Jesus, present in this Eucharist, give us strength and life with the spirit in ongoing resurrection of our martyrs, of all the martyrs of El Salvador famous or unknown, and may he bring us to personal consistency and to a commitment to the radical transformation of the world around us. So be it."

❄️   ❄️   ❄️

In an interview Tojeira was asked: What does the murder of the Jesuits mean for the El Salvador of 1993? "After four years one sees that the murder of our brothers has contributed to peace in El Salvador. It was like the drop of brutality which made the international reaction overflow. And this case has generated a great deal of truth within the country, leading people to speak the truth more freely. The public has seen how assassins have been supported by apparently respectable people in government and private business.... This death of my brothers and of Elba and Celina has helped many people to have the courage to speak the truth, to protest, and to confront the negative aspects of Salvadoran reality."[23]

❄   ❄   ❄

In his "letter to Ellacu" this year, Jon Sobrino told his dear friend that "things are not going well." The Truth Commission's report published in March was entitled "From Madness to Hope," but the country is now "in a difficult situation, one of more madness and less hope, a situation of crisis and tension." After assuring Ellacu that he and the other martyrs are very present and very deeply loved, Sobrino emphasized that in the midst of the crisis they have a very important message to give. "You keep alive the light, courage, and hope in all hearts of good will. And this is very necessary, because here, as in practically the whole world, they seek to deceive us and want us to forget what is fundamental: that this is a world of the poor and that, if we do not overcome poverty, there will be no important change."

Sobrino confessed that he is more and more struck by a "crazy idea" of Ellacuría, that the "solution and ideal for today's world is the **civilization of poverty**. To me that is the most revolutionary—and most Christian—thing you ever said. And it is something that practically nobody likes, beginning with ourselves who have a vow of

---

[23] *Carta a las Iglesias*, 16-30 de noviembre, 1993.

poverty. You remind the economists that the planet does not have sufficient resources for everyone to live like Europeans or North Americans, and so the latter must come down so that all can live. You remind the preachers and moralists of the First World that the society of abundance cannot be universalized, and so it is not and cannot be moral. And you remind the neoliberals and enthusiasts who think that history has reached its end point that we are going backwards, that there is now more poverty and greater inequality, and that we do not want this kind of society.

"You stated very prophetically that it is better to have no solution than to have a bad solution, that the United States is worse than we are because it has a solution but that solution is bad, both for them and for the world in general. The true solution is a civilization in which priority is given to labor rather than capital, which is what John Paul II also says. But you go further, adding that that civilization is one of poverty and that it is the only way of making the civilization of love a reality in history today.

"That civilization is the only one which can make life possible for all and which can generate spirit and humanity. You tell us, Ellacu, that it is better to live as poor people, but with creativity, celebration, community, commitment, faith, and hope, than to live in a routine way, with mere entertainment, with individualism, selfishness, pure pragmatism, and resignation. You tell us to live with spirit and not with the false self-complacency of those who think that the end of history has arrived."

Finally, Sobrino recalled that two months after the murders he was speaking on Spanish TV. "Remembering Jesus' words, I said 'never congratulate a millionaire.' Afterwards I thought of you, but I did not have the courage to demand the civilization of poverty, for fear that rocks would rain down upon me, and so I spoke of the 'civilization of shared austerity.'

"You see how you are missed, Ellacu. We miss your clarity, your compassion, your hunger and thirst for justice, your courage. May Archbishop Romero, Julia Elba and Celina, and you and your brothers grant it to us."[24]

Ellacuría had written of a poverty "which can enable all to have access to some material and cultural goods which would make for a truly human life. That poverty is what makes room for the spirit, which now will not be choked by the desire to have more than the other, by the concupiscent desire to have all kinds of superfluities, when most of humanity lacks what is necessary. Thus the gospel spirit will be lived out more easily, according to which it is not necessary to have much in order to be much; on the contrary, there is a limit at which having is opposed to being. There will be no place for avarice, which keeps people in insufferable work tensions just to store up more wealth in the quest for security or, what is worse, in the quest to be able to buy the will and morality of others."[25]

In the fall of 1993 the Jesuits at the UCA printed a hitherto unpublished article by Ellacuría in which he discussed the relation between the liberty of the rich and the liberation of the poor. "The bourgeois liberty which underlies much of the publicity about liberty is based on private property and more concretely on wealth; there can hardly be any talk of liberty without the imbalance between the few who have much and the many who have little. Bourgeois liberty, which

---

[24] *Carta a las Iglesias*, 1-15 de noviembre, 1993.
[25] Cited in *Carta a las Iglesias, ibid.*

presupposes liberation from the aristocracy and from the absolute monarchies, is founded on the oppression of large social classes which sustained without freedom the development of the bourgeois class. This is not Christian liberation/liberty.

"The gospel message sees in wealth a great obstacle to the kingdom of God and to the development of the freedom of the children of God. This point has been taken up strongly by most of the great religious reformers, who have seen wealth as the great obstacle to sanctity and have seen poverty, chosen out of love for Christ, as the great help to perfection. It cannot be denied, without suppressing essential elements of the gospel, that wealth is a great obstacle to Christian liberty and that poverty is a great support for that liberty. The idea of having more as a condition for being more is a diabolical temptation, rejected by Jesus at the start of his public mission. Today, however, it is presupposed that having more in the sense of having more than others is what makes it possible to be more and to be really free. Domination becomes the condition of freedom.

"In this way the gap between rich and poor, and between the rich and the poor peoples, becomes ever greater. That is why liberation as a collective process, whose principal subject (agents) are the poor, is the Christian response to the problem of collective freedom which in turn makes possible and enables personal freedom. There is no liberty without liberation; there is no Christian liberty without Christian liberation, and this has to do essentially with the poor and with poverty. It is the scandal which Christian faith should cause when confronting a world historically structured by sin more than by grace. While there are poor people, liberation will come from the poor."[26]

The interplay between personal struggle and collective history is an important issue for Ellacuría: "No sin, not even the most individual and interior, fails to have a repercussion in some way on the shaping of the person and on the march of history."[27]

In the same article Ellacuría also addressed the relationship between faith and justice: "Without confusing the two, faith and justice are inseparable dimensions, at least when both are found in their fullness within a world of sin. Christian faith in its fullness is not only the gift of self to God, the acceptance of his revealing communication, and the launching of a supernatural dynamism, but it is also a new way of life which necessarily includes the doing of justice; in its turn, doing justice is already a way of knowing God and of giving oneself to him, although perhaps without sufficient explicitation and clarity.

"But in any event it is clearer that there is no faith without justice than that there is no justice without faith. Nor should it be forgotten that a person can be saved without (explicit) faith while no one can be saved without justice. On the other hand, it is certain that the full truth of justice and consequently of justification cannot be attained except from faith. For example, only from the faith perspective can it be affirmed that (Christian) justice includes the preferential option for the poor, partiality in favor of the most needy."[28]

---

[26] "*Liberación*," unpublished text of 1987, published in *Revista Latinoamericana de Teología*, Septiembre-Diciembre 1993.

[27] *Ibid.*

[28] In the same vein, Rafael Diaz-Salazar wrote in the UCA's journal, *Estudios Centroamericanos* (June 1993), that "Christianity is a **religious** movement which, in contrast to others throughout the history of religions, is characterized by uniting

❋   ❋   ❋

On November 17 I celebrated Mass with a community of sisters who had known the martyrs well and had worked with them. The first reading of the day's liturgy, 2 Maccabees 7:1,20-30, was especially pertinent to the events we had been celebrating. "Seven brothers with their mother were arrested and tortured with whips and scourges by the king, to force them to eat pork in violation of God's law." The six Jesuits, brothers in the Lord, knew that their lives were in danger not because of faithfulness to dietary legislation but because of their faithfulness to the prophetic Word which God had put into their mouths.

The mother of the seven boys, far from urging them to cling to life as if it were an absolute good, exhorted them: "I do not know how you came into existence in my womb; it was not I who gave you the breath of life, nor was it I who set in order the elements of which each of you is composed. Therefore, since it is the Creator of the universe who shapes each man's beginning,...he in his mercy will give you back both breath and life, because you now disregard yourselves for the sake of his law." Hope in eternal life brings liberation from the fear of death.

After six of the brothers had died, the foreign king Antiochus tried to bribe the youngest with promises of honors and riches. The mother exhorted her remaining son in their native language: "Do not be afraid of this

---

consubstantially the adoration of God and the struggle for the liberation of the poor. Moreover, the Christian God himself [herself] is involved in that struggle, changing the poor into a sacrament of his presence and tying eternal salvation— the promise which is characteristic of all religions—to the struggle in history to liberate the oppressed (Matthew 25)." The author noted that the socio-political movements of the left share this central commitment to the liberation of the poor and thus can relate closely to Christianity.

executioner, but be worthy of your brothers and accept death, so that in the time of mercy I may receive you again with them." And her son reaffirmed his obedience to God.

The first six deaths, described in verses which are omitted in the reading, show the courage of the boys and their faithfulness to conscience, which is the real issue here. When one brother spoke out as the voice of the others, the king commanded his executioners to cut out his tongue, "to scalp him and cut off his hands and feet, while the rest of his brothers and his mother looked on." Still breathing, he was thrown into the fire. Such sadistic torture (in the presence of loved ones) has a contemporary ring to it for those who know the behavior of the Salvadoran troops, the Nicaraguan contras, and other U.S.-supported forces.

The second brother, scalped and at the point of death due to various tortures, said: "You accursed fiend, you are depriving us of this present life, but the King of the world will raise us up to live again forever." (The last brother called the king "wretch, vilest of all men.") The last words uttered by Ignacio Martín-Baró to his executioners were: "This is an injustice; you are rottenness."

The third "put out his tongue at once when told to do so, and bravely held out his hands, as he spoke these noble words: 'It was from heaven that I received these; for the sake of his laws I disdain them; from him I hope to receive them again.'" He is the patron saint of all who have been cruelly maimed for conscience' sake.

"The mother was last to die, after her sons."

In the Eucharist the sisters and I gave thanks to the Lord for all the martyrs of history and especially for the many courageous women among them.

＊   ＊   ＊

In an Advent editorial, *Carta a las Iglesias* emphasized that in spite of all the negative signs the fourth anniversary was celebrated "in a climate of joy, thankfulness, and hope, and in a commitment to struggle so that the blood shed and remembered may really bear fruit and be changed into new life for all. And this has been our experience: that hope is greater than despair, courage greater than fear, solidarity greater than individualism, generosity greater than selfishness, and work for peace greater than violent and murderous acts."

Three attitudes "which are necessary in this time of Advent" are: to hope, to prepare, to dream. "To **hope** against all hope. To hope, like the people of God in exile, when there seems to be no reason to hope or when experience seems to advise against hope as an illusion. To hope with the conviction that, in the midst of the apparent absence of God in our history and in our lives, God is indeed present and wants to be present through the actions of those whom he calls to be ever more human and to humanize the world more and more.

"To **prepare** the paths which can lead our Salvadoran society to a new reality in which there will be participation by all, in which there will be a multi-faceted leveling of conditions (solidarity including the economic dimension), dialogue among all forces to find the best solutions to our serious problems, respect and pluralistic acceptance of other ways of thinking as long as they are directed toward the common good, justice for all, the opportunity for everyone to live with dignity, etc.

"To **dream** that a society is possible in which we can really see the love of the Lord (as Psalm 85 says), in which his salvation comes to all of us, in which we listen to God who speaks to us of peace, in which grace and truth meet, in which justice and peace embrace and kiss with passion, in which truth springs forth from the earth and justice comes down from the heavens, in which justice walks before God and peace follows in his steps."[29]

❄   ❄   ❄

On December 26 the auxiliary bishop of San Salvador gave a year-end report in which he noted that in 1993 the archdiocesan human-rights office investigated 82 deaths attributable to death squads, almost twice the number of such cases in the two previous years. "It would seem," the bishop concluded, "that peace has not arrived. The people feel insecure, beaten by poverty and unemployment, and sometimes they ask what has been achieved by the signing of the peace accords in January 1992. It worries me that people are saying that things remain the same or are worse than before."[30]

❄   ❄   ❄

An editorial in the January-February 1994 issue of the UCA journal denounced two kinds of ongoing violence: political repression

---

[29] *Carta a las Iglesias*, 1-15 de diciembre, 1993.
[30] *Carta a las Iglesias*, 16-31 de diciembre, 1993.

and institutionalized injustice. "In 1993 the nation's press reported 1,217 violent deaths: 463 were attributed to common crime, 357 to unknown persons, 246 in circumstances which remain mysterious, 69 attributed to death squads, 68 to grenade explosions, and 14 attributed to security forces.

"Until investigations are carried out and evidence can be shown to the contrary, the assassinations by unknown persons and those in mysterious circumstances can be attributed to the death squads, in addition to the 69 assassinations attributed directly to these illegal groups. These statistics, however, should not lead us to forget the deeper reality. The ever wider and deeper poverty of El Salvador is the perennial problem, the one which gave rise to the repression and the war in the past, the one which is at the root of crime and social decay, and the one which blocks national reconciliation.

"While neoliberal economic policy generates wealth in a very reduced sector of the social pyramid, at the other extreme it continues to broaden and deepen poverty, whose most striking manifestation is the existence of hunger and sickness in the Salvadoran people. The wealth derived from economic growth in the last five years has benefited only a few.

"According to the Central Reserve Bank, in 1990 all salaries received amounted to 11.8 billion *colones*, while company profits came to 21.7 billion *colones*. In other words, approximately one and a half million salaried workers received 7,839 *colones* each, while about 20,000 business people took in more than a million *colones* each. Thus the average capitalist earned more than 127 times the earnings of the average salaried worker. Of each percentage point of economic growth, the capitalists take two thirds and the workers one third."[31]

❉   ❉   ❉

UCA president, Fr. Francisco Estrada, S.J., focused on this violence of injustice in his address on February 21, 1994, during the ceremony in which the university conferred an honorary doctorate on Congressman John Joseph Moakley. "Modern, highly technified sectors of society which maintain First World life-styles exist side by side with the majority whose minimal requirements for life go unsatisfied," he said. On the world scene, UN studies show that "one billion people in the Third World live, or barely survive, in absolute poverty, with 34 thousand children dying daily from malnutrition."

In Central America, "long before the majority is able to acquire what is necessary to live, the region is moving from a productive economy to one of speculation and consumerism. Capital has moved toward the financial system and the import sector, abandoning the productive areas of the economy. Our trade balance is increasingly negative, the only compensation being the remittances sent in by Salvadorans abroad and the earnings of workers in the export assembly plants."[32]

---

[31] *Estudios Centroamericanos* (ECA), p. 8.

[32] *Noticias SJ de la Provincia Centroamericana,* enero-febrero 1994. Estrada noted that Moakley was being honored for his defense of human rights in El Salvador and in particular for his work "in the declassification of documents which can offer proofs or leads as to who comprise and finance the deadly death squads" and for his work in the investigation of the UCA assassinations.

Just before receiving his honorary doctorate, Moakley (who has a picture of Archbishop Romero on the wall of his House office) visited the UCA chapel and prayed before the Jesuit martyrs' tombs.[33]

In his speech accepting the doctorate, Moakley urged the people to participate in the upcoming national elections, but added: "Voting is just one important step in a democracy. It is also vital that each and every one of you demands the full and faithful implementation of the peace accords that were agreed to over two years ago—and that includes the re-integration of former combatants from both sides into productive civilian life, judicial reforms, land transfers, the deployment of the National Civilian Police, and a sensitivity to human rights concerns.

"Elections lose their significance if other institutions that are key to a democracy are missing.

"You cannot have a true democracy unless you have a police force that is civilian based—free of the influence of the military. And, quite frankly, the suspension of the demobilization of the old National Police and the failure of the Salvadoran government to fully comply with the accords in building a new civilian police are very disturbing.

"You cannot have a true democracy unless you get serious about ending corruption in this country.... You cannot have a true democracy unless everyone—especially some former FMLN combatants— recognize that the old ways of armed conflict are over. There must be no more hidden arms caches and no more sinister plots for violence that endanger the delicate peace.... And you cannot have a true democracy

---

[33] *Carta a las Iglesias*, 16-28 de febrero, 1994.

unless you end impunity for those who engage in murder and intimidation....

Some have dismissed the recent spurt of assassinations as a mere consequence of a rise in street crime—and nothing more. They have said that the killings have nothing to do with politics.... Well let me suggest that when a congressional candidate is gunned down in broad daylight outside a nursery school and no robbery occurs—you can bet your life that's a political crime. Failing to acknowledge and forcefully condemn the obvious will not stop political killings. In fact, it will only give comfort to those extremists—whatever their ideology—to continue their cowardly and destructive behavior....

"It is so vitally important that this government—and all its institutions—demonstrate today what, in my opinion, they failed to do four years ago when the Jesuits were killed at this university, and that is: a willingness to confront hardline elements among its own supporters; a capacity to carry out a professional investigation; and an even-handed approach to the administration of justice."

Turning to his own country, Moakley said: "While I am proud of the role the United States played in conjunction with the United Nations in finally bringing the terrible war in this country to an end—I also know that my country must assume responsibility for much of the tragedy that occurred during the last thirteen years.

"The things we overlooked or chose not to see. The atrocities that official Washington chose to rationalize or explain away. The distortions and the excuses. The blind support of certain individuals—who deserved not our support but to be put in jail. And the contempt that some in my government had towards many who tried to tell the truth."

In order to avoid repeating the same mistakes, Moakley said, "last April I asked President Clinton to declassify all relevant U.S. documents pertaining to our involvement in El Salvador. To his great credit, the President agreed to comply, and many of those documents are now being made public...."

It is not enough to reveal the truth and name names, he said. "We must use the truth to make things better, to fix what is wrong, and to implement appropriate safeguards. The challenge for El Salvador and the challenge for the United States is to use the truth constructively—not merely rhetorically.

"I've often wondered whether we, in my country, could have pushed the day of peace closer here, in your country.

"What if we had frozen military aid after El Mozote? What if we had pushed harder and harder in the case of the murdered churchwomen? What if we had supported efforts by the Catholic Church for dialogue earlier—instead of insisting almost until the very end that a military victory was possible in this country? Could the war have ended sooner? We will never know."

❄   ❄   ❄

As El Salvador geared up for elections, an article in the UCA journal pointed toward the communities which functioned in FMLN-controlled areas during the war and the communities of returned refugees as fundamental sources of hope for a new kind of society. The vast majority of people in these communities see very clearly that "the struggle continues, that the only change has been in the way of carrying on the struggle, and that their greatest strength and their guarantee of success lie in their organization."

Popular culture in the communities promotes gospel values of justice and solidarity. Achievements of local development (e.g., a communal soup kitchen, a bridge, a cultural center) are celebrated in song, and an unjust tax increase is denounced in the music of protest. In one popular song the people express their hope that "government officials will work to improve conditions" and that "exploitation, indifference, self-interest, and egoism will disappear."

Life in these communities is characterized "by the practice of solidarity, cooperation, community, and celebration. These values, joined to new forms of ownership and production and to the democratic exercise of power, constitute the foundation of an authentic people's society."[34]

❄   ❄   ❄

In his Sunday homily on March 6, Archbishop Rivera y Damas gave some remarkably direct advice to voters: "A responsible vote must look toward the future, but the future we want cannot be built on foundations which are fragile or which are not seated on the firm rock of those values which guarantee a healthy society. How could anyone who thinks about the future vote for those who do not take the peace accords seriously? How could anyone who thinks about the future vote without adverting to the matter of who the killers of Archbishop

---

[34] Aquiles Montoya, "*La vida en las comunidades de la sociedad popular*," *Estudios Centroamericanos*, enero-febrero 1994.

Romero are and who organized the plot against his life and gave the order to kill him?" The archbishop recalled that those responsible for this vicious crime are still unrepentant.

"Whether they like it or not," he said, "the shadow of this sacrilegious crime stalks those who, even after fourteen years, remain unrepentant, idolizing the man who wanted to solve the problems of El Salvador with blood and fire. We say once again: the future of El Salvador cannot be built upon lies, arrogance, corruption, repression, hatred, and injustice."

He also noted that those involved in nominating candidates for the Supreme Court of Justice are guided more "by personal friendships, kinship, or, what is worse, by unmentionable personal interests" than by ethical reasons. It is clear to all, he noted, that the system of justice has been functioning badly.

That is why, the writers of this editorial noted, the Truth Commission made the unusual recommendation to remove the present Supreme Court.[35] The editorial continued: "Inspired by the gospel passage which warns against building a house on sand, Archbishop Rivera has come out clearly against voting for the ARENA party if people are concerned about El Salvador's future. [The Spanish word for sand is *arena*.] In the recent history of the country, no archbishop has ever said so directly that people should not vote for a specific political party (not to mention the party in power)....

"Rivera considers that the present government has gone to intolerable extremes and that a new government of the same party would put the future of El Salvador in serious danger.... If ARENA is

---

[35] *Proceso (UCA)*, March 9, 1994.

elected, the majority will continue in poverty, there will be no administration of justice, no democratization, the instruments which would guarantee respect for human rights will continue to be weakened, and national reconciliation will remain impossible.

"Such a clear and direct intervention of the archbishop against the ruling party is one of the most important new elements in these elections.... When it is true to the gospel, the Church always shuts the doors against those governments which are enemies of justice, truth, and peace. It shut the doors of the Milan cathedral against the Roman emperor until he made public penance." Thus it is not surprising "that Rivera has denounced the present government concretely for what it has failed to do and the ruling party for what it will not do if it is reelected." What the Church demands is not even in ARENA's platform. "The archbishop has been very careful not to mention the ruling party or its founder by name, but it was not necessary to do so."

The government was quick to react. "Undoubtedly disturbed by the archbishop's March 6 homily," the next edition of *Proceso* reported, "the government jammed the radio broadcast of his March 13 homily." The editorial, noting that in the past this kind of interference led to acts of violence, denounced this as a violation of freedom of expression.[36]

❄   ❄   ❄

Another problem with the electoral process was that thousands of Salvadorans had not been able to be registered as voters, especially in areas known to be pro-FMLN. In addition, voters in several pro-

---

[36] *Proceso (UCA)*, March 16, 1994.

FMLN towns in one region were told that they had to travel to the regional capital, Chalatenango, to cast their votes. This was interpreted as an attempt to discourage them from participating. In general, public transportation on voting day was severely reduced.

On March 20 thousands arrived at the polls with their voter cards only to find that they could not vote because their names were not on the official rosters. It was also discovered that over a thousand Nicaraguans living in El Salvador voted (illegally) after ARENA had promised them assistance.

In many polling places voting did not begin until 8 a.m., one hour late. They closed promptly at 5 p.m., however, leaving hundreds frustrated.[37]

These factors, plus a high degree of voter apathy, resulted in the fact that only fifty-three percent of potential voters actually cast their vote. (In adddition, pre-election surveys had indicated that only forty percent of the people believed the elections would be clean.) In the voting for president and vice-president, the ruling ARENA party received forty-nine percent of the votes, just short of the majority required for a new president. The left-wing coalition (FMLN, Democratic Convergence, and the National Revolutionary Movement) received 24.9%, while the Christian Democrats won 16.3%, with four other groupings sharing the rest.[38]

---

[37] *Carta a las Iglesias*, 16-31 de marzo, 1994.

[38] In the new Legislative Assembly, ARENA has 39 representatives, the FMLN 21, the Christian Democrats 18, and the PCN 4 (which ARENA can count on to give it a majority). As for mayors, ARENA won 206 positions, the Christian Democrats 29, and the FMLN 16.

Author and professor Renny Golden, an observer at the elections, wrote: "Unlike the defiant fraud of the past, ARENA's lieutenants did not openly cart off ballot boxes. They did not need to: the most determinative fraud was procedurally and legally accomplished during the voter registration period.... On election day, Salvadoran voters were confronted with army patrols in half the country's fourteen districts, the familiar silhouette of a machine-gun nest in the city of Chalatenango, an ominous buzz of helicopters in the former conflict zones, and roadblocks in Usulutan."

In the voting process itself, "ARENA supervisors and vigilantes (each party is allowed poll watchers) outnumbered, outmaneuvered, and overwhelmed opposition parties. Over the procedural objections of the FMLN supervisors, ARENA supervisors took down the voter registration lists posted over the voting tables, the only clear clue as to where voters were to vote, and posted them outside." In some cases ARENA vigilantes actually placed ballots in ballot boxes to 'assist' voters while the inexperienced and intimidated FMLN officials hovered over voter lists. Over four hundred Soyapango citizens who had registration cards were not on the voter lists. Missing completely at the vote counting that night were thirteen ballot tallies representing thousands of votes."[39]

Carta a las Iglesias reported that "in the UCA we had to explain to the foreign observers how it was possible that the victims voted for the executioners." After noting the high level of abstentionism, the authors quoted one voter as observing that people did not vote for the left coalition "because they were brainwashed. They were told that, if the Frente won, we would have to wait on long lines for shoes and beans, as in Cuba."

---

[39] "Elections in Salvador," *The Other Side*, May-June 1994.

Others believed right-wing propaganda that an FMLN victory would result in the closing of factories and other workplaces.

Moreover, many voted for ARENA out of a need for stability. Others, also thinking of stability, "did not vote for the left Coalition because they feared a violent reaction by the right in case of a leftwing victory." The country still does not offer a climate free of fear "where people can speak without anxiety about the taboo issues dealing with the great oppressors: the oligarchy and the military. There is still no climate for really free and just elections."[40]

Many felt that the lack of effective implementation of the Peace Accords deprived the elections of much of their potential. "As the UCA had been pointing out for some time, the interminable problems in the implementation of the Accords—specifically in the land-transfer programs, in deploying the new civil police, in the lack of compliance with the recommendations of the Truth Commission, and in the failure of the social-economic Forum—took political potential away from the elections."[41]

❄   ❄   ❄

---

[40] *Ibid.*

[41] *El Salvador Proceso (UCA)*, abril 13, 1994. *Envío* (UCA Managua, April 1994) pointed out: "With regard to the Peace Accords, we must remember that the negotiated solution to the war and the political formula which resulted from the Accords did not express the political will of the Cristiani government nor that of the powerful economic sectors which support ARENA. Rather, it was an outcome imposed by the national reality—influenced by, among other things, the FMLN's 1989 military offensive—and by international pressure which demanded a negotiated solution to the conflict. ARENA has complied with the letter but not with the spirit of the Accords."

March 24 marked the 14th anniversary of the assassination of Archbishop Romero. Jesuits at the UCA reflected on Romero and Ellacuría, noting that the death of each "significantly influenced the course of events.... With the death of Romero, war was unleashed; with the death of Ellacuría, peace was unchained."

Romero could not change the course of history. "He tried to exorcize the agents of evil with an appeal to their hearts: stop the repression. But those human hearts were already dried up, petrified, dead; far from softening with the message of Christian love, they became even harder; for the killers, Romero's every word proved anew how dangerous he was. Threatened, he refused to be intimidated and chose to offer his life for his people and for peace.

"However, what he wanted and intended was frustrated by the implacable dialectic of history: his death precipitated the war, immediately. With his death the situation was exacerbated, the indignation of the masses was rekindled, overwhelmed by the horror of the homicide and caught up in the whirlwind of violence. With the death of the archbishop the war became an inevitable necessity, like a blaze touched off in a dry wood by one match.

"The word of love and peace, the voice of reason, produced unconsciously and involuntarily its opposite effect. The goodness and holiness of Romero could do nothing, in his specific time in history, but unleash the demons, which managed to bury, in a wave of hatred, the prophet's message of Christian love.

"Nevertheless, his temporary failure appears later to be his true triumph: from the atrocious war, peace could finally be obtained, a peace more authentic, solid, and hope-giving than that which was achievable before the conflict."

Ellacuría saw that the time was right for serious peace negotiations. "Killing Ellacuría, shooting at his head, destroying that precious brain, his murderers sought to kill the peace-giving process of thought, nullifying the possibility of negotiation; they wanted to kill the negotiations. But they precipitated the opposite effect: they gave life to the negotiation process.

"It is no exaggeration to say that after their death the presence of Ellacuría and his murdered companions has grown larger, bursting through the borders of El Salvador, shaking consciences, changing attitudes, and motivating practical international actions which until then had been lacking. The irrationality of war left little room for reason; for more than a decade, time imposed the logic of destruction, the rule of fanaticism and intolerance. Only a few voices were raised in opposition to this tendency, among them that of Ellacuría. That voice was silenced, but in its own time it gained the victory."[42]

※   ※   ※

Since no candidate received a majority of the votes on March 20, a second round of voting was held on April 24 between the top two candidates. Official results showed that ARENA received 68.21% of the votes, while the left coalition won 31.78%. The abstention rate in this second round was fifty-five percent.[43] *Proceso* editorialized: "The most striking aspect of the elections continues to be the abstentionism, which is a repudiation of the Supreme Electoral Tribunal whose

---

[42] *Carta a las Iglesias*, 16-31 de marzo, 1994.
[43] *Proceso*, April 27, 1994.

inefficiency (whether culpable or not) ratified the people's lack of confidence in the elections and the electoral system."[44]

As the results became known, Ruben Zamora expressed satisfaction that his coalition had emerged as the second political force in the country and as a "firm alternative for development with social justice." Armando Calderon Sol, in his first statements, "surprisingly said that one of his priorities would be compliance with the Peace Accords." In the ARENA victory celebration, President Cristiani, "amidst vociferous shouts of 'fatherland yes, communism no,' reaffirmed the visceral anticommunism of the ARENA party in constrast to the more moderate tone of Calderon Sol's initial statements." Alluding to the left, Cristiani said: "Whether they like it or not, El Salvador will be the tomb where the reds will end up." Later the candidate elect recalled and gave thanks to the late Major Roberto D'Aubuisson for having passed on to them his ideals of "peace, progress, and liberty."[45]

In the midst of great international pressure, the Electoral Tribunal "managed to overcome some of the irregularities." More polling booths were set up, and transportation was improved. "However, April 24 saw a repetition of the problem of a lack of official electoral guides; ARENA took advantage of this situation by stationing its own guides who also distributed propaganda inside the voting places. Another problem which repeated itself was that of people who could not find their names on the list of voters."[46]

---

[44] *Ibid.*
[45] *Ibid.*
[46] *Carta a las Iglesias*, 16-30 de abril, 1994.

Why did some of the poor vote for the political project of the rich? "In the first place," UCA analysts noted, "many Salvadorans still believe in the phantasm of 'communism,' above all those of limited education. ARENA exploited this in its campaign.... In the second place, others probably based their vote on their immediate needs, thinking of their stomach. ARENA had promised some immediate partial improvements, and the people preferred an economic system which in the long run will leave them poorer than they are now."

Finally there is the factor called "the oppressor within." As part of the process of social control, "many of us end up interiorizing those values, ideals, and dreams of the oppressors which have nothing to do with our own reality."[47]

These analysts attributed the high rate of abstention to three factors: lack of confidence in the elections, lack of interest in the political process, and the level of conflict and polarization shown in these elections. With regard to the last factor, "veiled threats, uninvestigated deaths, and fears stimulated in the mass media" did not make for a nicely functioning electoral event. "In the end, the ghost of war seemed still present in the mind of the Salvadorans."

While noting the serious number of "irregularities" in the electoral process, *Carta a las Iglesias* also raised serious questions about the FMLN's showing. "Our FMLN, with 14 mayors out of a total of 262 and 21 representatives in an Assembly of 84, must ask itself seriously what happened and what happened to it. It is all too easy to blame the alienation of the people or the tricks of the adversary; what is needed is a profound analysis and self-criticism of the causes of the negative result." The editors also referred to the division within the ranks of the

---

[47] *Ibid.*

FMLN as evidenced by the controversial May 1 vote of some FMLN representatives in electing the Assembly leadership.[48]

The March-April 1994 issue of the UCA's *Estudios Centroamericanos*, devoted to an analysis of the elections, attributed the people's lack of confidence (not only in the electoral process but also in the governing system itself) partly to the government's failure to comply with the peace accords. The journal also raised some serious questions for the FMLN.

"As for the left, the people's loss of interest began when the left could not or would not oppose the right's rejection of the Truth Commission report, when it could not explain the arms deposits, and when the peace accords (including the reinsertion of ex-combatants in society) disappeared from its public agenda. And let us not forget that until recently the groups in power systematically besmirched the electoral process by their fraud, and the left, then rebels, denied the legitimacy of elections and in practice boycotted them."

The *ECA* editorial mentioned four mistakes of the left. The first was to concentrate too much on the presidential elections. "The second error was the lack of internal cohesion among the five parties of the FMLN, the Democratic Convergence, the National Revolutionary Movement, and their respective factions. Within the FMLN, the PRS-ERP [Salvadoran Revolutionary Party-Renewing Expression of the People][49] never accepted the candidacy of Rubén Zamora; rather, these groups sought to form a broad center to isolate ARENA. Moreover, the other FMLN parties criticized the PRS-ERP for supporting only its

---

[48] *Carta a las Iglesias*, 1-15 de mayo, 1994.
[49] The latter is the new name of the People's Revolutionary Army.

own candidates, ignoring the others. These circumstances led to a lack of consistency in the electoral propaganda.

"The third error was to impose some inadequate candidates in regional and local elections..., and the fourth was to accept ingenuously the so-called rules of the game, failing to denounce the way in which the electoral system was stacked against it."

The left's lack of a coherent and viable alternative political platform was also cited as a factor in its defeat. "What's more, the very notion of a new society seemed to disappear in the proposals of the left coalition, giving in to the logic imposed by ARENA." The FMLN, according to *ECA*, also lent support to its own demonization by some of its war tactics: transportation stoppages, electrical sabotage, blowing up of bridges, machine-gunning of cattle, burning of crops, car-bombings, etc.

Some factors favoring ARENA were the perception by some that the economy had begun to enjoy a "bonanza" since the end of the war and an expensive and effective propaganda campaign.

A pre-election poll conducted by the UCA's Institute of Public Opinion in February brought out some interesting aspects of the political situation. More than half of those interviewed expressed little or no interest in the electoral campaign. The vast majority also indicated that they had not participated in any political meeting and had no desire to participate actively in any party. This negative attitude was more pronounced among the peasant and marginal social sectors.

Asked whether poverty is the will of God, the majority said that it is not. However, more people of the lower economic classes said poverty is the will of God than did those of the upper classes. Similarly, more of the poor said that the situation of the country would not change (no matter what they did) than did the rich. The poor also had less confidence in the electoral process than the rich.

As for party preferences, the poll showed that, while the FMLN had stronger support among the poor than among the rich, it would not win in any social sector.[50] (The role played by fear in this response, as in the voting itself, must be seriously considered.)

The May-June 1994 issue of *ECA* editorialized on a somber note: "An armed conflict has come to an end, but its roots continue: an increasingly greater generalized poverty, the right to life and due process without protection, rampant impunity, and national reconciliation forgotten." The advances under the ARENA administration of the first part of the decade were due more to international watchdogs than to its own convictions. "Thus it is not far-fetched to think that when ARENA feels free of that international vigilance it may try to return to its old vengeful ways with impunity."

❄   ❄   ❄

Shortly before the March 20 first round of voting, Fr. Rodolfo Cardenal, S.J., vice-rector of the UCA, was asked to describe the progressive Church's priorities for after the elections. "The Church has a special mission," he said, "to help maintain the people's hope, to refocus things. It's not a matter of avoiding the problem but

---

[50] *Estudios Centroamericanos*, March-April 1994.

confronting it: to try to keep hope and a common vision alive in the people, something the FMLN is not doing either."[51]

On June 7 a Jesuit at the UCA wrote to the Jesuits of the United States: "The UCA Jesuits, along with others, received death threats yesterday, which were communicated to various news organizations. In addition, yesterday afternoon a woman phoned the theologate [seminary] community to warn: 'I want to tell you (pl.) that some Jesuits are going to die.' The caller hung up without waiting for a response.

"The two evening papers reported the threats (phoned to news organizations) on the front page. The two morning papers (associated with ARENA) did not. The El Mundo account read: 'Today a death squad threatened to murder, unless they should leave the country in 48 hours, the Human Rights Procurator...and other judicial functionaries, as well as Jesuit priests. The threat was made by a group calling itself the Domingo Monterrosa Commando Unit.'"[52]

The Commando Unit also threatened Juan Jeronimo Castillo "for running around investigating us," the voice said. The Jesuits were threatened "for getting involved in politics." Juan Jeronimo Castillo is a member of the Joint Group formed in December to investigate death squad killings which have taken place since the signing of the peace accords in January 1992.

On June 10 threatening calls were made to Archbishop Rivera y Damas and Bishop Rosa Chavez. Jesuit Jon Sobrino has said: "I will certainly stay in the country." Facing the threat "would be an important

---

[51] Interview by Paul Jeffrey, *Latinamerica Press*, March 31, 1994.
[52] Monterrosa was the commander of the Atlacatl unit which committed the El Mozote massacre in 1981.

message to the death squads, to show that we're firm, and to the people, so they won't feel they're abandoned when things get a little bit tough."[53]

Fr. Dean Brackley, a U.S. Jesuit and one of those who came to El Salvador to replace the murdered Jesuits, said the threats against the Joint Group's investigators "seem to indicate that (the Joint Group) is onto something, that it has rattled the cage of the sponsors of the death squads. That's a positive sign." Brackley's first reaction to the threat "is honestly to give thanks that the Jesuits here (keep) trying to unmask the official lies. I'm glad that they're still speaking the truth in the face of this kind of threat."[54]

---

[53] Article by Gene Palumbo, *National Catholic Reporter*, July 1, 1994.
[54] *Ibid.*

AFTERWORD

Those of us working as missionaries in what used to be called the Third World (now the world's South) are seeing nothing but deepening misery among our people. While about ten percent of the people of our countries are getting richer, and conspicuously so, the rest are struggling for the basics, with about fifty percent just barely surviving. Below that line, thousands of people, mostly children, are dying of malnutrition, diarrhea, cholera, and other diseases of the poor. The gap between the rich and poor of the planet, and that same gap within our countries and within the United States, widens.

In 1900 there were about one and a half billion people on earth. Presently we number 5 billion, and the UN estimates that by the year 2100 we will be 10 billion. If the current ratio continues, 8 billion will be living in poverty, with most barely surviving.

When I went to the United Nations in New York to get a copy of the Truth Commission's report on El Salvador, I spent some time sitting in front of the glass-encased "moon stone." My admiration for the technology which enabled humans to visit the moon and bring back some samples of material found there was coupled with a flight of fancy, imagining what technology could do to improve life on earth for all.

In the main lobby of UN headquarters I sat in front of a magnificent collection of poster-size pictures showing people from all corners of the globe (including a special exhibit on Vietnam). It felt natural to thank God our Father, the Creator of all peoples, for the efforts to form world community and to ask God to help us to go much further toward that true international fraternity which would be a sign of the coming of the Kingdom. May God's will, a world of justice, peace, and solidarity, be done. May all nations, and everyone in them, have their daily bread. Let real repentance and reconciliation, based on a new world order, flourish. Deliver us from the evils of individual and corporate greed and ethnic, nationalistic, and religious intolerance.

Several days later I went to North Carolina to show support for Philip Berrigan, Fr. John Dear, S.J., Lynn Fredriksson, and Bruce Friedrich, who were to be sentenced for pouring their blood and hammering on an F-15E warplane in one of the many Plowshares actions for peace. A major part of their message is that militarism is a sin and a crime against humanity because it kills the poor by causing them to starve, as the Vatican said years ago. One F-15E costs $50 million (one B-2 Stealth bomber costs over $600 million).[1] Five F-15E's would equal Nicaragua's entire annual export earnings.

How can we talk of hope? How can we rejoice in the coming of the Savior, when we know that two thousand years later the forces of greed and injustice are still killing Him in His beloved poor? We can talk of hope and joy today only in the measure that we cast our lot with the world's poor and oppressed and struggle with them for peace and justice on earth, as the Plowshares communities and many other peace and solidarity groups are doing. Instead of changing the channel to

---

[1] *The New York Times*, July 7, 1994, p. D3.

avoid seeing the starving of Africa or the oppressed of Haiti or the homeless in the wintry streets of the United States, let us allow reality into our hearts and minds. Let us stop the denial. Let us stop "keeping busy" in order to forget. Let us allow Christ in the world's poor to break open our hearts in compassion and solidarity.

At first it will be a downer. We will cry, curse, and be depressed. But we will be in touch with reality and truth, no longer alone on our island of wealth and toys. Benjamin Gonzalez Buelta, the Jesuit director of novices in the Dominican Republic, has written: "The oppression of the majority of our people is a scandal because it is happening in a Christian nation where oppressors and oppressed address God with the same prayers. The gap between rich and poor deepens every day. Those who begin to live in solidarity with the poor allow great rivers of pain to enter into themselves, affecting their deepest identity and their future plans. Those who look at such unjust misery will not be the same for the rest of their lives. That is why the prophets sometimes seem destroyed by the burden of solidarity under which they live.

"But at the same time we find that we are liberated by Christ. As we celebrate this experience with the poor communities, we find that their hymns have great truth in them, because they express their felt experience of liberation. Often, not having anything, they share as if they had everything. Suffering massacres, they receive a joy which defies all logic. Without schooling, they find a wisdom which allows them to pass through terrible storms. They really experience the joy of the beatitudes (Matthew 5:21) and happiness in fraternal service (John 13:17), with the joy of the Risen One reflected in their faces (Philippians 4:4). Liberation is born in the midst of oppression. Jesus looked at oppression and denounced it. But he also saw the Father in those situations, working to free people (John 5:19-20), and he joined that work of liberation rising up from the heart of oppression (*La Transparencia del Barro*)."

The truth will set us free. We will quickly find other Americans in the same process of truth-seeking, trying to get free of the cultural blinders, trying to experience some reality therapy. Together, we will say "no" to the TV commercials and to the social pressures; our only status symbol will be the quality of our friendships and the depth of our commitment. We will move toward a life-style which is not so parasitic and predatory on the rest of humanity. We will join in social and political struggles to defend our human rights (e.g., against environmental pollution of all kinds) and the rights of the poor in the States and in other countries.

How to begin? First of all, we must *see* reality from different angles, not just from that of our political, economic, and media establishment. Don't flip the channel in that rare moment when the world's pain enters your living room, but don't rely on the big networks to show you how it was today. Look for books and magazines which present alternative views. Travel: to the poor in your own city or county or to the poor who are the majority in the countries of the world's South.

Secondly, *judge* how our wealth and consumerism affect the majority of the human race. Consider environmental destruction, unequal terms of trade between the industrialized countries of the North and the raw-material-producing ones of the South, the deadly but immensely profitable weapons industry, the foreign debt of the poverty-stricken peoples, the various kinds of intervention in recent history to prevent or destroy revolutions. What does it say about us as

Christians in the United States that just a little over one percent of our federal budget goes to foreign aid for the rest of the world, while about thirty percent still goes to our military system?

Thirdly, *act* to free yourself from complicity in the evil of the system. Strive for downward mobility in your lifestyle. If your work is a meaningless and self-destructive rat-race, stop running; find something that makes sense in terms of using your talents in service of people, and spend more time with your family and friends, nature and art. Work for justice. As the prophet Micah summed it up: "Act justly, love tenderly, and walk humbly with your God."

On my return visits to the States, people often ask me whether I suffer "culture shock" at the sight of vast abundance and waste in comparison to the deprivation in Central America. While the contrast remains striking, what I find more shocking is the spiritual and personal devastation among our people, especially among the young. Lack of meaning, lack of purpose, lack of challenge perhaps account for the fact that "drinking to get drunk" has tripled among college students in the last ten years. Suicide among the young is also an astounding phenomenon.

Vaclav Havel, president of the Czech Republic, has stated: "We enjoy all the achievements of modern civilization that have made our physical existence easier in so many important ways. Yet we do not know exactly what to do with ourselves, where to turn."[2]

Kairos/USA, a project involving many U.S. Christian groups committed to justice and to discerning the signs of the times, has noted

---

[2] "The New Measure of Man," remarks upon receiving the Philadelphia Liberty Medal at Independence Hall on July 4, as published in *The New York Times*, July 8, 1994, p. A27.

Holiday Inn

fax to :
P. Dean BRACKLEY, S.J
011-(503) 273-5000

re March 24.

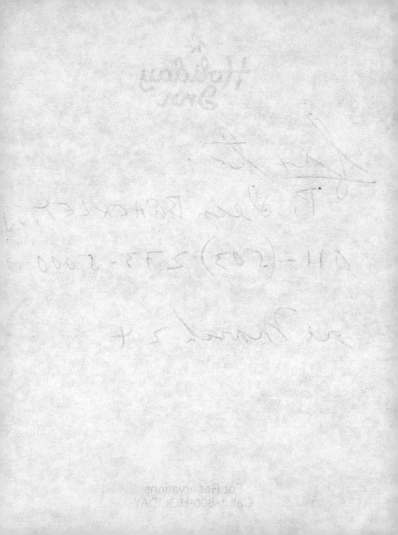

that "social oppression and cultural breakdown are the twin signs of
our age. One has to do with structural injustice; the other, with the
collapse of values.... There is a vast emptiness in this land, a lack of
moral vision, a dullness of spirit which the scriptures call hardness of
heart....

"Our shopping-mall culture keeps consumers busy in an age of
hitherto unknown materialism whose signs are emptiness, loneliness,
anxiety, and a fundamental loss of meaning. A most revealing sign of
the times is the blank, sad, or angry looks in the eyes of the young who
congregate both on the wasting corners of our urban mean streets or in
the wasteful corridors of our suburban shopping centers....

"The 1980s witnessed the largest transfer of wealth in human
history from the impoverished Southern hemisphere to the already
enriched North, largely in the form of interest payments on the debt. A
similar transfer took place in the United States from poor and working
class citizens to the upper 5% of the population. In the United States
the vast majority of people who are poor are full time workers or their
dependents. The fact that worldwide 40 million people die from
hunger-related causes each year and that one of every four U.S.
children is born in poverty is a serious challenge to those who would
accept the economic status quo."

In the third world "enforced austerity measures and structural
adjustments squeeze the life out of people. In our own country we see
cities which are similarly jammed, their mortgages held elsewhere. But
oddly, even among the affluent, we recognize the certain 'enslavement'
of those who have sold themselves onto the treadmill of credit card
bondage, nearly oblivious that they have thereby bound themselves in

servitude to a system."[3]   The Kairos document challenges us to become free of servitude and meaninglessness by following the way of the gospel. "When he disembarked and saw the vast crowd, his heart was moved with pity for them, for they were like sheep without a shepherd; and he began to teach them many things" (Mk 6:34).

In Nicaragua in 1993, the Ecumenical Committee of U.S. Church Personnel decided to fast one day a week, starting with Advent and continuing through 1994 and perhaps indefinitely, in solidarity with the Nicaraguan people in their deepening misery. "We also see this as a step toward simplifying our life-style in view of today's global realities and toward renewing our commitment to struggle for justice," the missioners stated. "A constant theme in our meetings and prayer sessions is the increasing impoverishment of the peoples of Latin America and the Caribbean and the growing poverty in the U.S. We are profoundly saddened to see how Christmas is celebrated in a way which buries the message of 'good news to the poor.'" The group invites people in the United States to join in the fast, which includes a commitment to have direct contact with the poor and to work for justice.

---

[3] "On the Way: from Kairos to Jubilee," Kairos/USA, (Pentecost 1994). Copies of this 24-page document may be ordered from Pax Christi USA; 348 E. 10th St; Erie, PA 16503. Tel: (814) 453-4955.

APPENDIX ONE

The Blood of the Martyrs Brought to The White House
and
A Visit To U.S. Army School Of The Americas

On January 5, 1990, Philip Berrigan and I poured blood on the gateposts of the White House while twenty-seven other demonstrators held poster-size photos of the butchered bodies of the Jesuits killed in El Salvador the previous November. One of our banners presented our main message: "Stop Aid to the Salvadoran Army and the Contras." As a result of this act of civil disobedience, I spent one day in jail and was sentenced to time served.

Others in the group, who had fallen on the sidewalk to represent the victims of U.S. policy, or who knelt in prayer, were also arrested and released on their own recognizance.

The blood was our own, mixed with some of the blood-soaked earth from the yard of the Jesuit residence in San Salvador where the six Jesuits were massacred. I felt confident that my brother Jesuits would have wanted their blood to be used in this way: with profound reverence for the life it represents and in an effort to contribute to life and peace and justice in their beloved El Salvador.

When I went from Nicaragua, where I had been working for four years, to El Salvador for the funeral, I saw the blood-soaked yard and blood-stained floors of their house. I saw the blood and brains which had been spattered from the yard onto the outer wall of their residence. I saw the brain matter and the dried blood which had flowed from the room where the cook, Elba Ramos, and her daughter Celina were murdered.[1] All Americans should view that blood, I felt, because the blood shed by the Jesuits and by thousands of others in El Salvador is on the hands of the U.S. government, which has supported the murderous military. I brought to the United States pictures of the yard, the wall, the blood, the destroyed bodies, and the extensive damage done by heavy weaponry to the pastoral center (with the Salvadoran army surrounding the university).

We made the blood of the priests visible at the White House, because the Bush administration supported the Salvadoran military which had killed not only these Jesuits but thousands of other civilians through indiscriminate bombing of the countryside, strafing of urban neighborhoods, "extra-judicial" executions, and disappearances.

---

[1] Spattered blood and brains have been the sign of massacre for centuries. An Indian document at the time of the Spanish conquest described the slaughter: "Roofs have been torn from the houses; their walls are bloody red. Streets and squares are crawling with maggots; the walls are stained with brains." (Miguel León Portilla, *El reverso de la conquista: relaciones aztecas, mayas e incas*, Mexico 1987, p. 53, as cited by Rivera Pagán, *op. cit.*, p. 434.

Our action was no desecration of the Jesuits' blood or of the White House. The desecration was done to them, other Christs, whose bodies were temples of the Holy Spirit, and that abomination was paid for by U.S. tax dollars. As for the White House, the blood of some of its victims, manifest close up, may cleanse and redeem not only its residents but other members of the government, if they have eyes to see. We fervently hope that the blood of these martyrs will open the eyes and soften the hearts of America and bear fruit in a new policy.

Our blood and the blood of the martyrs also represented the gallons of blood shed in Nicaragua by the U.S.-supported contras. I traveled on pastoral mission through the central mountains where the contras operated (and some remnants still function), and I saw the fear and dread they put in the eyes of the poor farmers. To some extent I felt that fear myself. The fear was not chiefly of death, but of being viciously tortured. The contras frequently slit the throats of their victims, watching them bleed and die like cattle.

I have celebrated numerous Masses for the soldiers killed by the contras and for some of the contras' civilian victims. I have also celebrated a prayer service for a contra who had been killed. And I celebrate Mass regularly in the rehabilitation hospital in Managua with civilians and soldiers who have lost limbs or been paralyzed by contra land mines or bullets.

Blood can be a sign of life, or of death. It can also represent redemption, conversion, healing, change.

❄   ❄   ❄

The group statement began with the same words used by the Berrigans and others in the draft-file burnings of the sixties: "We apologize, dear friends, for the fracture of good order." The statement continued: "We mean no insult or injury to anyone, but we must make the truth visible in order to save human lives in Central America and to awaken human consciences in our own country.

"The mountains of El Salvador have been the killing fields of government repression for years, and in November the same government bombed and strafed urban neighborhoods to quell the revolution, violating the human rights of innocent civilians. A wave of persecution of the churches ensued, with many church leaders and workers being arrested and some forced into exile because they work to bring the Good News of justice to the poor.

"In Nicaragua the mountains are wet with the blood of thousands of poor farmers who have had their throats slit by the U.S.-supported contras.... In Panama hundreds of civilians were killed and many more wounded in the latest expression of U.S. gunboat diplomacy: the illegal invasion to topple an unpopular and corrupt dictator."

The protestors, whose action took place on the vigil of the Epiphany, further stated: "The visitors from the East had been questioned about the Savior by a jealous and ruthless ruler who in his paranoia ordered the slaughter of the innocent children. Today the Epiphany of the Lord, the Liberator of the oppressed, is manifest in the struggles of the poor for a decent life, for a peace based on justice. 'If they kill me, I will rise again in the Salvadoran people,' said Romero. That epiphany is once again accompanied by the martyrdom of the innocent, as Jesus is crucified and rises again in his people....

"We apologize, dear friends, for the fracture of good order. But until that 'good order' is a just and peaceful world order, we will struggle to change it, so that blood may be a symbol of life and not of cruel torture and death. May the new year inaugurate a new decade of Good News for the poor in the U.S. and throughout the world. Let us begin by stopping the blood-letting."

❄   ❄   ❄

37 Arrested In Capitol Rotunda

On January 23, 1990, immediately after an interfaith prayer vigil and rally on the steps of the Capitol attended by hundreds of Church representatives from various parts of the U.S., 37 persons entered the rotunda of the Capitol to bring a message to Congress. Among them were members of various Catholic religious orders, a legislative expert for a Jewish agency, and a Lutheran pastor.

Under the huge dome of the Capitol, eight people lay down on the floor, covered by sheets bearing the names of various categories of victims of U.S.-sponsored repression by the Salvadoran government: peasants, indigenous, health workers, children, religious workers, and others.

Actor Martin Sheen proclaimed the group's statement, calling on Congress "to end military aid to El Salvador and to support a negotiated political settlement." Others knelt in reverence for the victims and in prayer for peace. Some read aloud the 1980 letter of

Romero to President Carter demanding a cut-off of U.S. military aid; others read the 1967 speech by Dr. Martin Luther King, Jr., in which he named the U.S. government "the greatest purveyor of violence in the world today" and called for an end to counter-revolutionary interventions around the world.

The eight "bodies" on the floor were dragged off by arresting police, while others participating were also taken into custody and charged with "unlawful entry" and "demonstrating in the Capitol building."

In his brief trial statement Philip Berrigan asked the judge to investigate U.S. foreign policy, adding: "If you do so, perhaps you will join us in taking action to change it."

U.S. Army Instructors Discuss El Salvador

In December 1989 I visited the U.S. Army School of the Americas at Ft. Benning in Columbus, Georgia. According to a Fact Sheet published by the School, "since 1947 the School has graduated more than 46,000 officers, cadets, and noncommissioned officers from 22 Latin American countries." In recent years El Salvador had the largest number of soldiers in training at the School, with 52 Salvadoran cadets graduating in 1990.

I talked at length with two civilian professors and an officer who has served as a military advisor to the Salvadoran Army. They plainly stated their conviction that elements of the Salvadoran military killed the six Jesuits and the two women on Nov. 16. "When they secure an area," said one staff member, "they do it right. And the killers not only got in but apparently were in no hurry to leave."

They considered it "possible" that the idea of the crime might have been mentioned to someone at "the station" (CIA) or the U.S. Embassy and that some indication might have been given that such a deed would not result in serious action by the U.S. government. (Indeed, U.S. Major Eric Buckland testified in early January 1990 that he had received prior knowledge of Col. Benavides' desire to kill the Jesuits at the UCA.)

The three staff members believed that the crime was committed by members of the Salvadoran Army's First Infantry Brigade, under the command of Col. Francisco Elena Fuentes. Col. Elena Fuentes is known as a hard-liner who has long wanted to take a no-holds-barred approach to putting down the insurgency, they said. "Give me the money and I'll clean up this country" is how one staff member characterized Elena Fuentes's attitude. With the ARENA party in power and with "weak signals" coming from Washington on human rights, Elena Fuentes had a green light to act as he saw fit, they said. (As it turned out, these staff members were correct in accusing the Salvadoran military but mistaken in pointing the finger at the First Infantry Brigade instead of the Atlacatl Battalion.)

When the Salvadoran guest instructor at the School heard of the killing of the Jesuits, he expressed sadness but said that they were helping the communists, the subversives. This was the reaction of most Salvadoran students at the School, according to staff members.

My conversation partners referred to President Alfredo Cristiani as "Freddy" and consider him a "puppet" of the Salvadoran military. They considered Roberto D'Aubuisson (now deceased), the founder and leader of the ruling ARENA party, responsible for the killing of Archbishop Romero. One of the staff members noted that D'Aubuisson reportedly was heard talking about the killing of Romero before it happened and then boasting about it afterward. They said that D'Aubuisson's class, the *Tandona* (which means large graduating class), monopolizes power in the Salvadoran military.

They described Vice-President Quayle's visit to El Salvador earlier in 1990 as a laughing-stock. At one point he brandished a weapon but held it pointing at himself. His message about human rights was seen as lip service. One staff member said: "If the Bush administration had given stronger signals of opposition against human rights abuses, the Jesuits would not have been killed."

They characterized as a "wrong signal" the fact that the head of the U.S. Military Group in El Salvador is a Salvadoran-American, Colonel Milton Menjivar. The Salvadoran military see him as one of their own, they indicated.

I showed my conversation partners a copy of the leaflet which was dropped from helicopters over San Salvador and which is identified by the emblem and name of the Salvadoran Air Force. It tells people that they have a perfect right to defend their lives and property and that if, in order to do that, they have to kill FMLN members and their "international allies," they should do it. When I asked the staff members whether this seemed authentic, they read the message and immediately responded: "This sounds just like Gen. Bustillo," then head of the Salvadoran Air Force.

I noted that according to the report of *Tutela Legal*, the human rights office of the Archdiocese of San Salvador, Elba Ramos was shot in the vagina. "That's typical of the death squads," said one staff member.

When I mentioned the Jennifer Casolo case (a church worker then in jail on the charge of hiding weapons on her property), they simply smiled and said that the Salvadoran military needed a case like this to divert attention away from the killings of the Jesuits and to back up their claim that foreigners and other church workers were collaborating with the FMLN.

When I observed that Lucia Barrera, a witness to the killing of the Jesuits, had been forced by interrogators in Miami to change her report of what she had seen, the staff members said that interrogators have all kinds of techniques to confuse witnesses.

During the course of the visit, I recalled what Dom Helder Camara, then Archbishop of Recife, Brazil told me in 1978: "Latin American military students learn the more sophisticated methods of torture at the School of the Americas." I asked one staff member how the issue of torture is handled at the School. "First of all," he said, "the School does not have to teach torture techniques. The students already know them. As for approving or disapproving, it all depends on the teacher's body language." When I asked for clarification, he said that a teacher might say "you can't use torture" but might add "but you really have to get the information," and wink.

This staff member also stated emphatically that a frequent response by the students to any talk by teachers of respect for human rights is: "How can you tell us about human rights after dropping the atomic bomb on Japanese cities?" He noted that many Latin Americans studying at the School have a simplistic view of the opponents to their government. "They are either with us or against us, and if they're against us, they're communists and we destroy them," characterizes this attitude.

Although the international communist bloc has disintegrated, Western hemisphere military leaders still speak of dangerous threats which they must be prepared to destroy. Retired Gen. Hector Gramajo, one of the Guatemalan Army's most notorious human rights violators[2], was the guest speaker at the School of the Americas graduation in 1991. "Comparing the current state of communism to a dragon, Gramajo said the crumbling of the Berlin Wall signaled the beheading of the dragon; however, its tail is still poised to deliver a devastating blow to the countries of Latin America."[3]

Col. José R. Feliciano, commander of the School of the Americas, has called Gramajo a "brilliant individual" and has accepted Gramajo's suggestion to train Latin American officers to perform civilian duties as well as military ones.[4]

General Edwin Burba, former Ft. Benning commander and now the four-star head of all U.S. deployable forces, has cautioned against any further "hemorrhaging" of the Pentagon budget. "My budget in Forces Command has been cut by one-third," he told the Kiwanis Club of Columbus, Ga., in 1992. "We must be careful not to cut too far. It is

---

[2] See "Hector at Harvard," by Dennis Bernstein and Larry Everest, Z Magazine (July/Aug. 1991). This article describes Gramajo's crimes against humanity as detailed in a "30-page, multi-million dollar federal lawsuit" prepared by the Center for Constitutional Rights on behalf of Guatemalan victims and their families. Amnesty International, Americas Watch, and other human-rights organizations have condemned Guatemala's military record under former Minister of Defense Gramajo. The lawsuit was served on Gramajo just before he received honors as a graduate from Harvard's John F. Kennedy School of Government in June 1991.

[3] The Bayonet (Ft. Benning newspaper), Jan. 3, 1992.

[4] The Benning Patriot, Feb. 21, 1992.

still a dangerous world. The threats are there, we just don't know where they are."[5]

Burba's Commander-in-Chief would say during his ill-starred campaign: The Soviet bear may be dead, but there are still a lot of wolves out there.

The belief in unspecified threats and wolves helps to cushion the impact of peace. "Despite the end of the Cold War and President Bush's pledge to curb overseas weapons sales, the United States has become the world's leading arms merchant," the same edition of the Benning Leader reported in a story taken from wire reports. "America's arms exports to the Third World have risen from $4 billion in 1986 to $14 billion last year, according to the Congressional Research Service. The United States now supplies more than half of all arms sold to the Third World.

"Pentagon suppliers seek eased export restrictions and more help from U.S. officials in marketing their weapons abroad. 'It's understandable that the goals of the U.S. defense industry are to hold on to old markets, open new ones and be capable of competing freely with foreign defense industries,' a top State Dept. official told the U.S. Defense Trade Advisory Group. Doing that, said Assistant Secretary of State Robert Gallucci, means 'the resulting economic prosperity will be good for the whole nation.'

"This year the Pentagon plans to supply arms and military aid worth $32.7 billion to 154 of the world's 190 nations."[6]

"Nineteen of the 27 Salvadoran officers whom a U.N. Truth Commission report implicated in the Jesuit murders were graduates" of

---

[5] *The Benning Leader* (Columbus, Georgia.), October 23, 1992.
[6] *Ibid.*

the School, according to *Newsweek* (Aug. 9, 1993). The defendants in the case had been taught by U.S. military trainers not only in the Nov. 1990 course in El Salvador but previously in various courses in the United States.[7]

Forty eight of the 69 Salvadoran officers cited by the Truth Commission for human rights violations are graduates of the School of the Americas.[8] Rep. Joseph Kennedy offered an amendment to the Defense Appropriations bill for FY94 which would have cut funding for the School; the amendment was defeated by a vote of 174 to 256, which suggests that ongoing political education about the School could result in termination of its funding.

From April 11 to May 20, 1994, people across the United States participated in various ways in the "Forty Days for Life" campaign to close the school. Hundreds converged on Washington to lobby their representatives to support Rep. Kennedy's second attempt to end funding for the school. Many fasted and reflected with Fr. Bourgeois and ten others who held a 40-day, juice-only fast on the steps of the Capitol. Kennedy's amendment was defeated by a vote of 175 to 217, with 46 abstaining.

The *National Catholic Reporter* noted that "retired U.S. Army Major Joseph Blair, who taught logistics at the School of the Americas from 1986-1989, said four-hour blocks of instruction on human rights

---

[7] See Doggett, *Death Foretold*, p. 47.
[8] Central America Working Group Legislative Update, Oct. 14, 1993.

awareness were given while he was on the faculty, but described them as 'a bunch of bullshit.' Blair said one class he sat in on was taught by a Chilean army officer, 'a Pinochet thug.' Human rights for most Latin American soldiers are 'a joke,' Blair said. They associate human rights with subversives, primarily the Catholic Church and groups such as Amnesty International."[9]

The article quoted former Marine Corps commandant Gen. A.M. Gray in a 1990 article from the Marine Corps Gazette: "Our superpower political and military status is dependent upon our ability to maintain the economic base derived from our ability to compete in established and developing economic markets throughout the world. If we are to maintain this status, we must have unimpeded access to these markets and to resources needed to support our manufacturing requirements."[10] Fr. Bourgeois found that to be a good summary of the School of the Americas' mission.

Momentum continued to grow. On June 16, the 206th Presbyterian General Assembly adopted a resolution calling on President Clinton, Congress, and other national leaders to close the school.[11]

---

[9] *National Catholic Reporter*, April 8, 1994.

[10] As quoted in *Brave New World Order* by Jack Nelson-Pallmeyer (Orbis, 1992). At the start of the July, 1994, summit meeting of leaders of the seven major industrial nations, *The New York Times* (July 8, 1994) observed: "the biggest problem faced by the industrial democracies is no longer tariffs. It is how to protect their intellectual property—books, software, movies, patents, and videos—from pirates in developing countries; how to get more access for their service industries like insurance, banking, brokerage and consulting; and how to lower barriers and provide more guarantees for the billions of dollars in investment capital flowing from the industrial world to the emerging economies of Asia and Latin America."

[11] *S.O.A. Watch* (Summer 1994).

APPENDIX TWO

The Massacre at El Mozote

The following are excerpts from the UN Truth Commission report on the massacre at El Mozote:

Village of El Mozote

"On the afternoon of 10 December 1981, units of the Atlacatl Rapid Deployment Infantry Battalion (BIRI), arrived in the village of El Mozote, Department of Morazan, after a clash with guerrillas in the vicinity.

"The village consisted of about 20 houses situated on open ground around a square. Facing onto the square was a church and behind it a small building known as the 'convent' used by the priest to change into his vestments when he came to the village to celebrate mass. Not far from the village was a school, the Grupo Escolar.

"When the soldiers arrived in the village they found, in addition to the residents, other peasants who were refugees from the surrounding areas. They ordered everyone out of the houses and into the square; they made them lie face down, searched them and asked them about the guerrillas. They then ordered them to lock themselves in their houses until the next day, warning that anyone coming out would be shot. The soldiers remained in the village during the night.

"Early next morning, 11 December, the soldiers reassembled the entire population in the square. They separated the men from the women and children and locked everyone up in different groups in the church, the convent and various houses.

"During the morning they proceeded to interrogate, torture and execute the men in various locations. Around noon, they began taking out the women in groups, separating them from their children and machine-gunning them. Finally, they killed the children. A group of children who had been locked in the convent were machine-gunned through the windows. After exterminating the entire population, the soldiers set fire to the buildings.

"The soldiers remained in El Mozote that night. The next day, they went through the village of Los Toriles, situated 2 kilometres away. Some of the inhabitants managed to escape. The others, men, women, and children, were taken from their homes, lined up, and machine-gunned.

"The victims at El Mozote were left unburied. During the weeks that followed the bodies were seen by many people who passed by there. In Los Toriles, the survivors subsequently buried the bodies.

Background

"The Atlacatl Battalion arrived at El Mozote in the course of a military action known as 'El Rescate,' which had begun two days earlier on 6 December.... The Atlacatl Battalion was a 'Rapid Deployment Infantry Battalion,' or 'BIRI,' that is, a unit specially trained for 'counter-insurgency' warfare. It was the first unit of its kind in the armed forces and had completed its training, under the supervision of United States military advisers, at the beginning of that year, 1981."

The report notes that earlier the Atlacatl troops had suffered a humiliating defeat at the hands of the guerrillas, having "to withdraw with heavy casualties without achieving its military objective."

The goal of *Operacion Rescate*, the report continues, "was to eliminate the guerrilla presence in a small sector in northern Morazan." Other instances of torture and murder by Atlacatl forces are described.

Subsequent Events

"The El Mozote massacre became public knowledge on 27 January 1982, when *The New York Times* and the *Washington Post* published articles by Raymond Bonner and Alma Guillermoprieto, respectively, reporting the massacre. In January they had visited the scene and had seen the bodies and the ruined houses.

"In the course of the year, a number of human rights organizations denounced the massacre. The Salvadoran authorities categorically denied that a massacre had taken place. No judicial investigation was launched and there was no word of any investigation by the Government or the armed forces."

In October, 1990, criminal proceedings were initiated. "The remains were ordered exhumed, and this provided irrefutable evidence of the El Mozote massacre. The judge asked the Government repeatedly for a list of the officers who took part in the military operation. He received the reply that the Government did not have such information."

The Results of the Exhumation

The exhumation of the remains in the ruins of the little building known as the convent, adjacent to the El Mozote church, took place in November 1992. "In the laboratory, the skeletal remains of 143 bodies were identified, including 131 children under the age of 12, 5 adolescents and 7 adults." The average age of the children was approximately 6 years. One of the victims was a pregnant woman.

"The weapons used to fire at the victims were M-16 rifles. As the ballistics analyst described, '245 cartridge cases recovered from the El Mozote site were studied. Of these, 184 had discernible headstamps, identifying the ammunition as having been manufactured for the United States Government at Lake City, Missouri.... All of the projectiles except one appear to have been fired from United States-manufactured M-16 rifles.'

"At least 24 people participated in the shooting. They fired 'from within the house, from the doorway, and probably through a window to the right of the door.' An important point that emerges from the results of the observations is that 'no bullet fragments were found in the outside west facade of the stone wall.'

"The experts...reached the following conclusion: `All these facts tend to indicate the perpetration of a massive crime, there being no evidence to support the theory of a confrontation between two groups.'

Findings

"There is full proof that on 11 December 1981, in the village of El Mozote, units of the Atlacatl Battalion deliberately and systematically killed a group of more than 200 men, women and children, constituting the entire civilian population that they had found there the previous day and had since been holding prisoner."

After naming officers in command of the Atlacatl Battalion at the time of the operation and identifying other massacre sites, the Truth Commission asserted: "Although it received news of the massacre, which would have been easy to corroborate because of the profusion of unburied bodies, the Armed Forces High Command did not conduct or did not give any word of an investigation and repeatedly denied that the massacre had occurred." The Commission cited the Chief of the Armed Forces Joint Staff at the time, who "was aware that the massacre had occurred and failed to undertake any investigation.

"The High Command also took no steps whatsoever to prevent the repetition of such acts, with the result that the same units were used in other operations and followed the same procedures." The Commission also named the President of the Supreme Court of Justice of El Salvador, Mr. Mauricio Gutierrez Castro, who "has interfered unduly and prejudicially, for biased political reasons, in the ongoing judicial proceedings on the case."

❄   ❄   ❄

In its December 6, 1993 issue, *The New Yorker* published a long, detailed article by Mark Danner entitled "The Massacre at El Mozote."[1]

While much of the blame for the Salvadoran army's "dirty war" was laid to the death squads, "there can be no doubt that the 'dirty war' was basically organized and directed by Salvadoran Army officers—and no doubt, either, that the American Embassy was well aware of it," the author emphasized. He interviewed Howard Lane, the public-affairs officer in the Embassy from 1980 to 1982, who said: "There was no secret about who was doing the killing—except, maybe, in the White House." The administration claimed it was a mystery in order to placate Congressional concerns about governmental violations of human rights.

Colonel John Cash, a U.S. military attaché, told Danner: "The Salvadoran officers used to brag to me that they didn't take prisoners."

---

[1] In 1994 this article was expanded and published as a book, *The Massacre at El Mozote*, by Mark Danner (New York: Vintage Books).

Lt. Col. Domingo Monterrosa Barrios, commander of the Atlacatl Battalion, sought to give his elite troops a certain mystique. "They shot animals and smeared the blood all over their faces, they slit open the animals' bellies and drank the blood," a lieutenant in another unit told Danner. Atlacatl troops celebrated their graduation "by collecting all the dead animals they could find, boiling them together into a bloody soup, and chugging it down." Then they sang the unit's theme song: "We are warriors! We are going forth to kill a mountain of terrorists."

One of the original American advisers with the Atlacatl told Danner that El Mozote was in a zone that was totally controlled by the guerrillas. "You know you're not going to be able to work with the civilian population up there, so you just decide to kill everybody," he said. While the zone may have been controlled by the guerrillas, the fact is that El Mozote was not a guerrilla town.

After carrying out a similar massacre in a nearby town, the men of the Atlacatl heard their captain counsel: "What we did yesterday, and the day before, this is called war.... And, goddammit, if I order you to kill your mother, that is just what you're going to do."

After the army left the area, the FMLN troops moved in, finding bodies everywhere. Reports reached the Archdiocesan human-rights agency, which contacted the Rev. William L. Wipfler, who was the director of the human-rights office of the National Council of Churches, in New York. He contacted Ambassador Deane Hinton, demanding information about the reported massacre.

Danner suggests that the ambassador had probably already received reports of a massacre; "after all, no fewer than ten American advisers were working with the Atlacatl at the time." According to one of them, members of the Military Advisory Group at the Embassy had telephoned an Atlacatl base within a few days of the massacre, saying they wanted Monterrosa to come in to talk. The American adviser told Danner: "Monterrosa just climbed into his helicopter and said, 'If they want to talk to me, I'll be out with my troops.'"

In mid-December Todd Greentree, the junior reporting officer at the Embassy, was invited by the FMLN to visit El Mozote. "I was convinced that something had gone on, and that it was bad," he later said. The ambassador refused to allow Greentree to go, saying it was too risky and that Greentree would just be playing into FMLN hands.

On January 3, 1982, Raymond Bonner of *The New York Times*, along with photographer Susan Meiselas, entered the Morazán region of El Salvador when the FMLN agreed to their persistent requests. In El Mozote they saw bodies, parts of bodies, and gutted houses. Bonner interviewed Rufina Amaya, an eyewitness to the El Mozote massacre. The guerrillas gave Bonner a list of seven hundred people who had died in and around El Mozote.

Alma Guillermoprieto of *The Washington Post* arrived in Morazán ten days later and saw bodies "mummifying in the sun." On January 27 the two reporters' articles, with photos, began to appear in print. Within two days, Pres. Reagan told Congress that the government of El Salvador was "making a concerted and significant effort to comply with internationally recognized human rights."

On Jan. 30 Greentree, along with Maj. John McKay of the U.S. military attaché's office, were taken by the Salvadoran Army to Morazán. But the main goal of the U.S. Embassy was not to have a thorough investigation of the massacre. "The primary policy objective at the time was to get the certification through," Greentree told Danner, referring to the Reagan administration's campaign to convince Congress of human-rights progress in the recipient country.

McKay told Danner: "In general, we had very little cooperation [from the Salvadoran military] when we went to Morazán." As the helicopter approached El Mozote they saw some destroyed buildings but were reportedly shot at from the ground. After returning to a military base, the Americans interviewed some displaced persons in a refugee camp. However, the Americans were accompanied by a squad of soldiers. "You had a bunch of very intimidated, scared people, and now the Army presence further intimidated them," McKay said. (This tactic was also repeated in the Jesuit case, when an eyewitness, who had been taken to Miami for her security, was questioned by the FBI in the presence of a Salvadoran military officer.)

Greentree managed to talk to some people without the military escort but still noticed a very high level of fear. He did not get any direct eyewitness accounts. Nonetheless, the interviews "convinced me that there probably had been a massacre, that they had lined people up and shot them," he told Danner.

Greentree and McKay set out once again, this time in a military jeep, but as they neared El Mozote the sergeant in charge said: "We're not going any farther, we're not going to help you." McKay said: "It was made very clear that we would get no more cooperation." The investigation was over. Greentree remembers thinking as he returned to the capital: "If we're really going to get to the bottom of this, there's going to have to be a decision to put a tremendous amount of energy into it, to carry out a more formal investigation, like the ones conducted for the Americans"—the four churchwomen. No such decision was ever made.

Although the investigation was obviously inadequate, Greentree wrote his report, and the next day the Embassy sent a cable to Washington which formed the basis for the administration's report to Congress. The cable claimed that the Embassy investigation "of reported massacre at El Mozote" included a "visit to the area." The summary continued: "Civilians did die during *Operación Rescate* [Rescue] but no evidence could be found to confirm that Government forces systematically massacred civilians in the operation zone, nor that the number of civilians killed even remotely approached number being cited in other reports circulating internationally."

Danner observes: "What is curious is how, instead of building on their observations, inferences, and conclusions to present the best version possible of what **probably** happened, [the Embassy investigators] emphasize the gap between what could be **definitively** proved to have happened—which, of course, wasn't much, given the reticence of the people and the constraints on the investigators' movements—and what the newspapers and the guerrillas were claiming had happened."

Had he not been operating under the constraints of politics in Washington, what would he have written differently? "Well, I would have put in more strongly the impression that abuses against the civilian population probably took place in El Mozote and the surrounding areas during that operation," Greentree acknowledged.

The cable concludes by noting that the defense attaché's office "is attempting to determine which Army units were present in El Mozote during and after the operation." If the Embassy wanted to discover the truth, it could have put the question "directly to the American-funded and American-trained Army," Danner notes. "And yet six weeks after the events were alleged to have taken place the Embassy reported that it had not managed to discover which units were in El Mozote—this although at least ten American advisers were assigned to the Atlacatl, the unit accused in all the press reports."

Shortly after sending the cable, Hinton himself questioned how it was being used by the State Department. On February 1 he cabled Washington: "I would be grateful if Department would use extreme care in describing my views on alleged massacre." It seems that Washington had been saying that the Ambassador, in his reply to the National Council of Churches, had denied the massacre had taken place. "My letter did not 'deny' incident: it reported that at that time I had no confirmation and...had no reason to believe Venceremos [guerrilla radio] reports. I still don't believe Venceremos version but additional evidence strongly suggests that something happened that should not have happened and that it is quite possible Salvadoran military did commit excesses." The Department held fast to its line, however, that the human-rights situation, while horrendous, was becoming less horrendous.

On February 10 the *Wall Street Journal* attacked Bonner's reporting on El Mozote as "overly credulous." Other criticism came from the Embassy, the State Department, and various right-wing publications. In August the *Times* took Bonner off the Central America beat and assigned him to the Metro desk in New York. While the executive editor of the *Times* denied caving in to pressure, in Danner's view the decision "to remove a correspondent who had been the focus of an aggressive campaign of Administration criticism no doubt had a significant effect on reporting from El Salvador."

In 1984 Col. Monterrosa, who was the commander of the Atlacatl Battalion in 1981, was asked by James LeMoyne what had happened in El Mozote. "We carried out a *limpieza* [clean-up operation] there," he said, as LeMoyne reported to Danner. "We killed everyone. In those days, I thought that was what we had to do to win the war. And I was wrong." Shortly thereafter, Monterrosa was exuberant when his troops captured the Venceremos Radio transmitter. Flying over an area near El Mozote with his prized trophy which he was going to show off to the media, the man responsible for the massacre down below in 1981 perished when his helicopter turned into a "great orange-and-black fireball." His trophy had contained a powerful FMLN bomb.

In July 1993 the Secretary of State's Panel on El Salvador, created in the wake of the Truth Commission report, concluded that the Department's handling of the massacre investigation "undermined the Department's credibility with its critics—and probably with the Salvadorans—in a serious way that has not healed.... A massacre had indeed occurred and the U.S. statements on the case were wrong."